CH

BFI FILM CLAS

. . . .

Edward Buscom.....
SERIES EDITOR

Cinema is a fragile medium. Many of the great classic films of the past now exist, if at all, in damaged or incomplete prints. Concerned about the deterioration in the physical state of our film heritage, the National Film Archive, a Division of the British Film Institute, has compiled a list of 360 key films in the history of the cinema. The long-term goal of the Archive is to build a collection of perfect showprints of these films, which will then be screened regularly at the Museum of the Moving Image in London in a year-round repertory.

BFI Publishing has now commissioned a series of books to stand alongside these titles. Authors, including film critics and scholars, film-makers, novelists, historians and those distinguished in the arts, have been invited to write on a film of their choice, drawn from the Archive's list. Each volume will present the author's own insights into the chosen film, together with a brief production history and a detailed filmography, notes and bibliography. The numerous illustrations have been specially made from the Archive's own prints.

With new titles published each year, the BFI Film Classics series will rapidly grow into an authoritative and highly readable guide to the great films of world cinema.

Poster for Part I of *Olympia*

BFI FILM
CLASSICS

OLYMPIA

·····················

Taylor Downing

BFI PUBLISHING

First published in 1992 by the
BRITISH FILM INSTITUTE
21 Stephen Street, London WIP IPL

British Library Cataloguing in Publication Data

Downing, Taylor
Olympia
I. Title
791.4372

ISBN 0-85170-341-0

Designed by
Andrew Barron and Collis Clements Associates

Typesetting by
Fakenham Photosetting Limited, Norfolk

Printed in Great Britain by
The Trinity Press, Worcester

CONTENTS

· ·

ACKNOWLEDGMENTS

Although this is only a short book there are several people who have contributed towards it. Firstly, my thanks to the staff of the National Film Archive, especially Anne Fleming, Elaine Burrows and David Meeker, for their help in copying the film and with many research queries. Markku Salmi checked the film credits. Thanks to the Department of Film at the Imperial War Museum and to Roger Smither, Paul Sargant and Jane Fish, who allowed me to look through their files on the history of this remarkable film. Thanks also to Lutz Becker, who has spent many hours in conversation about Riefenstahl and her films. But most thanks, again, to Anne for all her help and encouragement.

Leni Riefenstahl prepares her 'Manuscript' beforehand

INTRODUCTION
· ·

In assessing most films, there is a clear line of analysis to follow. A film is produced in a particular genre by a director and a team of creative artists working under a specific economic production process. When the film is completed it is released and can be judged and evaluated in its own right and alongside other movies from the same genre. After some years the movie may become a 'classic' or may largely be forgotten.

None of this applies to Leni Riefenstahl's *Olympia*. To start with, there are many *different* films which Riefenstahl made about the 1936 Berlin Olympic Games. There were five different-language versions of the film produced in 1938, some of which had a more 'positive' view of Hitler than others. In 1938 and 1939, versions of the film were received with great acclaim throughout much of Europe and it won first prize at the Venice Film Festival. But the war transformed the history of the film. Prints were seized by different military authorities and after the war they became subject to the provisions relating to enemy property. Censors cut the film. Distributors made their own versions. After the war Riefenstahl was imprisoned by the Allied military authorities, who investigated her as a possible war criminal. In consequence, Riefenstahl herself severely cut the film when it was re-edited for approval by the German authorities in 1958 as part of the process of her own 'de-Nazification'. But there are still several different versions of the film in archives around the world. Possibly none of the versions is the same as that first shown in Berlin in April 1938 at the gala premiere on Hitler's birthday.

As far as the production of *Olympia* is concerned, Riefenstahl has given her version of the circumstances under which it was made. But documents available in the German state archives suggest a different story about its financing and production. These are not mere academic differences. The relationship between the film, the film-maker and both the Nazi Party and the Reich fundamentally affected the way the film was made and its purpose and objectives. Is the film a piece of Nazi propaganda? Or is it one of the best sports documentaries ever made? Is it primarily about sport or about politics? Obviously, to a degree, it is about both and yet it transcends both.

It is impossible to assess *Olympia* without seeing it against the history of previous Olympic films. In this context the film's true originality becomes clear. But the film must also be seen in the context of film-making in Nazi Germany. How independent was Riefenstahl from the Nazi Party and, specifically, the Propaganda Ministry of Dr Joseph Goebbels? This is a central question to any appreciation of the film. And, of course, Riefenstahl's work cannot be isolated from the event of the Games, which were far and away the most spectacular Olympic Games held to date. This is only a short book but it attempts to sketch out this backdrop before going on to analyse the film in some detail.

The National Film Archive version of *Olympia* at least has a clear pedigree. It is copied from a print of the film given on permanent loan by the Imperial War Museum in April 1959. The film had been deposited at the Museum by the Army Kinema Corporation after the war. The AKC copy seems to have been the full English version of Riefenstahl's film. It derives from a copy that was held in the German Embassy in London in September 1939 and was seized by the authorities on the declaration of war. This book is about *that* version of

Leni Riefenstahl editing her film

the film, which as far as is known is Riefenstahl's original English version.

The English version with the original English-language commentary runs 19,608 feet, that is, 218 minutes. The original German version, called *Olympische Spiele*, ran for an extra seven minutes. The major difference appears to be that it gave slightly longer coverage to the Opening Ceremony. There might also have been some extra shots of Hitler in the German version, although this is not known for certain. Also, all the different-language versions included extra sequences of sportsmen and women who were of particular interest to the country where that version was to be screened. These differences probably account for the missing minutes. There have been other German versions since, including Riefenstahl's own post-war shorter version. This book will deal only with the version which is available in Britain. The English-language version has always been called *Olympia*. Therefore, this book has the same title.

I have filmed through two Olympic Games (Seoul and Barcelona). I know what it's like. All the best laid plans go wrong. The most detailed preparations are overtaken by unexpected events. Nothing goes as planned. Everything changes. Regardless of everything I write over the following pages I have the greatest admiration for anyone who can get what they want out of filming an Olympic Games – even if it means staging events beforehand or re-shooting them afterwards, as Riefenstahl and her crews did in liberal measure. Whatever conclusions are reached about *Olympia*, to have shot the footage which Riefenstahl captured in Berlin is a great achievement that should never be underestimated. Believe me.

I
....
THE OLYMPICS ON FILM 1896–1932

The cinema and the modern Olympic movement were born at the same moment of time. In June 1894, a young French aristocrat and intellectual, Baron Pierre de Coubertin, called a gathering of sports leaders from around Europe to a meeting in Paris. In the grand setting of the Palace of the Sorbonne it was resolved to establish the International Olympic Committee with the purpose of reviving the ancient Olympic Games. Two years later, in April 1896, 295 athletes gathered in a brand-new marble-lined stadium in the centre of Athens to celebrate the first Olympic Games of the modern era. Meanwhile, also in Paris, in December 1895 in the basement of the Grand Café, the Lumière brothers gave what is usually regarded as the first public performance of the 'cinématographe' to a paying audience.

It is curious that two phenomena which have become such powerful social and cultural forces in the twentieth century should have had their genesis at the same moment towards the end of the nineteenth. A hundred years later the story of the moving image and that of the Olympic movement have become closely bound together. For television, the child of cinema, the Olympic Games now offer a huge spectacle. Today the Games are viewed live by an estimated five billion people in almost every nation around the globe. As one NBC executive put it, 'The Olympic Games are simply the biggest show on television. There is nothing else like it.'[1] The Olympics have offered the cinema and television one of the best opportunities to attract a vast audience, and repeatedly the Games have been used to showcase new techniques and advances in styles of television presentation.

But the connection between the moving image and the Olympic Games, so powerful by the end of the twentieth century, has not always been thus. Although the Lumière brothers sent out 'opérateurs' with their camera-cum-projectors to shoot actuality film all over Europe and even in Russia, they entirely missed the first modern Olympics held amid much razzmatazz before a crowd of 80,000 in Athens in the spring of 1896. There is no known film record of the first, historic modern Games. Although there is film shot many years later which purports to show the Games, it is not authentic.[2] There is some footage of the

Universal Paris Exposition of 1900, alongside which the next Games were held; and footage also exists of the St Louis World Fair of 1904, in which the Olympic Games nearly got lost amid the sideshows and fringe events. By the time of the London Games of 1908, the Olympics attracted the interest of the newsreel or 'topical' companies. Much footage was shot of this splendid event, held at the brand-new White City stadium in west London. The newsreels helped to make an international hero out of Dorando Pietri, the marathon runner, who staggered into the stadium ahead of the other runners but was helped across the finishing line by officials, a friendly gesture which led to his disqualification, all recorded on film.

The first Olympics to receive serious attention on film were the Stockholm Games of 1912. These Games were known for the efficiency of their organisation and for their friendliness of spirit. Hours of material were shot. However, this footage does not seem to have been released at the time as a complete film but rather as a series of newsreels or news features.[3] The Olympic Games were now sufficiently strong to survive the trauma of war and the cancellation of the Berlin Games of 1916. When the war came to an end Antwerp, in the heart of devastated Belgium, was chosen to represent the rekindling of the human spirit by the Games. Despite the rhetoric of universality, the defeated powers were not invited to participate.

Up to this point, the film record of these early Games is of greater interest to the Olympic historian than to the historian of film. None of the footage lays any claim to cinematic achievement. The fixed camera angles, the lack of camera movement, the predominant use of wide-angle lenses were all characteristic of the newsreel cameraman and no lessons were learnt from the great classics of the silent cinema that by the 1920s was in its heyday. Nor is there any evidence that any of the great cinema pioneers of this time, like D.W. Griffith or Fritz Lang, showed any interest in filming the Games.

The 1924 Games were the first which were marked by the production of a full-length feature-type film. A two-reeler was made by Rapid Film of the first ever Winter Games, held in Chamonix, France. A much longer, ten-reel film of the Summer Games in Paris was made by the same company. This film delightfully captures the spirit of these Games, in which Harold Abrahams won gold in the 100 metres and Eric

Liddell, the 'flying Scot', took a surprise gold in the 400 metres with a world record (events later memorialised in the film *Chariots of Fire*). Paavo Nurmi of Finland began his sensational Olympic career by winning four gold medals. All the principal events are recorded in the film, each followed by a portrait of the winner, still puffing, face-on to the camera. The film is also of interest in that it attempts to illustrate the range of Olympic events, including the swimming, gymnastics and equestrian sports, in addition to track and field events in the main stadium. The film runs over two and a half hours and was edited in two versions, one with French and one with English titles. This film, produced by Jean de Rovera, lays claim to being the first Olympic feature although we know little about its production or about the film-makers behind it. In the scale of its coverage of the Games, the 1924 epic is a hint of things to come.

Most film and sport historians usually claim, mistakenly, that the first Olympic feature film was made by Dr Arnold Fanck (of whom more later) about the 1928 St Moritz Winter Games. The film was called *Das weisse Stadion* (*The White Stadium*). It was slightly shorter than the average feature. It had the full official backing of the IOC but was a low-budget affair, funded by UFA, the German film production and distribution company. Only two cameramen worked on the film and Fanck was allowed seventeen days to edit the material. He was assisted in the cutting room by Walter Ruttmann. Although Fanck was a director best known in Germany for his mountain films, he seemed to have no heart for this opportunity to evoke the grace and agility of the world's best winter sports competition. He is reported to have said that all that was necessary to produce a documentary was to be present at an event and to film it. Predictably, the resulting film was mediocre and uninspiring.

Despite the example of the 1924 Paris Olympics film, there was no official film made of the 1928 Amsterdam Olympics. Even more surprising is the lack of any major film of the 1932 Games in Los Angeles. The dazzling new Coliseum Stadium was only a few miles from the heart of the worldwide cinema business in Hollywood, but the film industry once again largely ignored the event, despite the fact that competitors from thirty-eight nations and a million and a quarter spectators made the Los Angeles Olympics one of the greatest events ever staged in the city. During the competition sixteen world records were broken and thirty-three new Olympic records were set, and the United States emerged as the dominant force in the sprint events.

Although there were some attempts to put together an Olympic film, for one reason or another they all came to nothing. The only surviving evidence of interest shown by the movie moguls in the world's greatest sporting event happening just up the road derives from a decision by an executive from Universal Studios to send a team to film what they could of the Games. The Universal cameramen set up their equipment at the back of the stadium and filmed events in long shot. Their one fascinating contribution to the history of film and the Olympics was that they carried out the first synch-sound interviews with Olympic winners. These were filmed trackside after an event, anticipating television by fifty years. Unfortunately, when the Games were over and the cameramen brought back their footage, no one at Universal seems to have had the slightest idea what to do with it. The film survived, some of it still not processed, in the Universal vaults until it was rediscovered in the 1970s. It then formed the basis of the production of a later Olympic film-maker, Bud Greenspan, in his reconstruction of the Los Angeles Games. As an interesting movie footnote to the Games, it was in 1932 that Johnny Weissmuller, who had won five gold medals in swimming events in the previous two Olympics, started to appear as Tarzan in the movies produced at MGM. Here, at least, the aura of Olympic gold spilled over into the world of the silver screen.

So, after forty years of Olympic history, by the time of the 1936 Berlin Games any film-maker interested in shaping the Olympic Games into a film of feature proportions had very little precedent to draw upon. It is at this point that the remarkable and ambitious Leni Riefenstahl enters the frame. Never would Olympic film-making be the same again.

II

·························

RIEFENSTAHL BEFORE 'OLYMPIA'

Leni Riefenstahl was born Helene Bertha Amalie Riefenstahl on 22 August 1902 in Berlin. Her father owned an engineering firm and she grew up in a prosperous environment in which, unusually, she was not encouraged to view life as a journey through marriage to motherhood and the life of a *Hausfrau*. Her father wanted her to train for business but her mother had great artistic ambitions for her, possibly out of a sense of her own unfulfilled creative talents. Her mother prevailed and Leni started dancing lessons from the age of eight. She later joined the famous classical Russian Ballet School in Berlin, where she began to excel. Attracted by the new school of dance associated with Isadora Duncan, Leni trained with one of Duncan's pupils, Mary Wigman, in Berlin. She seemed to revel in the natural expression of her body through dance and she loved to perform in loose garments, barefoot on stage without scenery or props.

By 1920, Riefenstahl was dancing regularly in the major cities of Germany, and over the next few years she travelled throughout central Europe earning high fees. At about this time she met Dr Arnold Fanck and began her career in film. Fanck (who later produced the 1928 St Moritz Winter Games film) was a wealthy geologist who in the 1920s used his fortune to establish a genre of mountain adventure films which was almost of equal importance to the German cinema of the time as the Western was to the American cinema. In 1924 Fanck was looking for a leading lady to appear in his next film when he saw Riefenstahl perform. Fascinated, he signed her up to appear in his new film *Der heilige Berg* (*The Holy Mountain*). Riefenstahl was immediately infatuated by the otherworldly appeal of the mountains, which seemed to release a great creative passion within her. She was also entranced by the medium of film. Fanck believed that no genuine mountain film could be produced in a studio and he made all the actors and technicians endure the rigours of working at altitudes above 12,000 feet. In this setting Riefenstahl was in her element. In the male worlds of mountaineering and film-making she clearly impressed Fanck and his team with her vigour and her determination.

In all, Riefenstahl starred in six of what became Fanck's most famous films, including *Der grosse Sprung* (*The Great Leap*) in 1927, *Stürme über dem Mont Blanc* (*Storms over Mont Blanc*, also known as *Avalanche*) in 1930, *Der weisse Rausch* (*The White Frenzy*) in 1931 and *SOS Eisberg* (*SOS Iceberg*) in 1932. Today the best-known of these mountain films is the classic *Die weisse Hölle vom Piz Palü* (*The White Hell of Pitz Palu*), co-directed by Fanck and G.W. Pabst in 1929.

Riefenstahl has often asserted that she learnt a lot about film technique from Fanck, whom she questioned repeatedly during filming. Of Fanck and his team she said, 'I never stopped watching, observing, asking questions'.[4] In the mountain films Riefenstahl often played the part of a young girl representing the innocence, purity and harmony of the mountain people in contrast with the decadence and greed of late Weimar German society. Later critics, especially Siegfried Kracauer in *From Caligari to Hitler*, have seen in the heroic idealism and the Promethean grandeur of these films a 'mentality kindred to the Nazi spirit'. Certainly an obsession with the healthy outdoors, with the titanic struggle against the supreme forces represented by rocks and glaciers, has some parallels in Nazi thinking. But at this stage the mountain films probably represented to an audience more than anything else a sense of escape from a world dominated by economic distress, rising unemployment and falling living standards.

Riefenstahl's fascination with mountains led her to direct her first feature film, *Das blaue Licht* (*The Blue Light*), which she also produced, wrote and starred in. In 1931 she set up an independent production company with Hans Schneeberger, the cameraman on many of Fanck's films with whom Riefenstahl was having an affair, and with Béla Balázs, the Hungarian writer. The film was made in the stunningly beautiful setting of the Saarn valley in the Dolomites. Schneeberger and Riefenstahl used every device to add to the natural beauty of the location, including soft focus, time-lapse photography and graded filters on shots of mist, dawn and sunshine. Light and shadow were used to powerful effect. In the film Riefenstahl played the part of Junta, a wild outcast girl who shepherded goats. The story was little more than a simple melodrama in which Junta falls in love with a visiting Viennese painter who tries to befriend her when all the other villagers spurn her. But the film shows in Riefenstahl and the small team she built around her the potential of a film-maker of ambition and power.

The Blue Light was released in Germany in the spring of 1932, and one of those greatly impressed by the film was Adolf Hitler, leader of the National Socialist Party. The Nazi Party was well known for the thuggish behaviour of its supporters and its fervently anti-Jewish and anti-communist stance. But at this time Hitler was still keen to make the Party appear respectable since he saw the route to power as being through the ballot box. In January 1933 Hitler was made Chancellor, and the Nazis began the seizure of total power which overwhelmed the fragile, democratic German state and was to change the course of twentieth-century history. But when the aspiring political leader first met the ambitious and glamorous young film star and director, all this was in the future.

There is considerable mystery about exactly when Riefenstahl and Hitler first met and in what circumstances. Most probably they first met in 1932 after the success of *The Blue Light* had given Riefenstahl a certain notoriety and when Hitler was on the threshold of power. One of the crucial questions about Riefenstahl centres on her relationship with Hitler. Was she a Nazi and did she become Hitler's lover? She always claimed later that she was politically naive, that she knew nothing of Nazi ideology and cared even less for it but that she admired

Leni Riefenstahl in *Das blaue Licht*

Hitler as a good man. She never actually became a member of the Party, which, on one level, certainly could have helped her career. Later she claimed that it was the incompetents and thugs around Hitler who perpetrated the crimes of the Nazi regime and that Hitler himself knew nothing of these crimes. The cry of ignorance is of course the familiar plea of those tainted with accusations of guilt. But no assessment of Riefenstahl can fail to address the often repeated claims that she was Hitler's lover, that her promotion within the Nazi regime was due to her relationship with the Führer, and that she was far closer both to Hitler and to the Nazi Party than ever she admitted later.[5]

In this context it is interesting to quote at length from a witness of the first supposed meeting between Hitler and Riefenstahl, as recounted in the post-war memoirs of one of the Führer's 'set' at the time, Ernst 'Putzi' Hanfstängl. At this time, before Hitler seized power, Hanfstängl believed the best way to restrain him was to introduce him to attractive female companions who would in some way humanise him. Hanfstängl is regarded as a reasonably reliable witness and it is known that at this time some of the Nazi leaders thought it would be a good thing for Hitler to have a lover. Hanfstängl reveals that it was in fact Goebbels and his wife who made the first introduction:

About the only thing which reconciled me to the Goebbels was their unashamed enthusiasm for finding female companionship for Hitler. I was all in favour of this. I thought if he could find another woman it would be the best way of taming him and making him more human and approachable. Leni Riefenstahl was [one] of the Goebbels' introductions. She was in their apartment one night for dinner.

Leni Riefenstahl was a very vital and attractive woman and had little difficulty in persuading the Goebbels and Hitler to go on to her studio after dinner. I was carried along and found it full of mirrors and trick interior decorator effects, but what one would expect, not bad. There was a piano there, so that got rid of me and the Goebbels, who wanted to leave the field free, leant on it chatting. This isolated Hitler who got into a panic. Out of the corner of my eye I could see him ostentatiously studying the titles in the bookcases. Riefenstahl was certainly giving him the works.

Every time he straightened up or looked around, there she was dancing to my music at his elbow, a real summer sale of feminine advance. I had to grin myself. I caught the Goebbels' eye as if to say, 'If the Riefenstahl can't manage this no one can and we might as well leave.' So we made our excuses, leaving them alone, which was against all the security regulations. But again it was an organised disappointment. The Riefenstahl and I travelled in a plane a day or two later and once more all I got was a hopeless shrug. However, she had made her mark and obtained quite a lot of privileges from Hitler for her film activities.[6]

After his mother's death, women played only a marginal role in Hitler's life. The world he inhabited from 1914 onward was that of the barrack room, the beer hall and the almost exclusively masculine setting of the Nazi Party, in which there was not a single prominent woman. Much has been written about Hitler's coldness, his stiffness and his inability to relate to others in conventional human terms. He was relaxed only in the company of his cronies. With regard to women, at this time he still seems to have felt inhibited and he had a great fear of being compromised. He was also still suffering grief in the wake of the suicide of his niece, Geli Raubal, the year before. It seems unlikely, therefore, that in 1932 Hitler would respond to any sexual approaches. Later, he liked to surround himself with pretty women who were good at social talk. Eva Braun, his mistress for many years, was at the centre of this social scene.

Riefenstahl seems to have won the genuine admiration of Hitler. He certainly respected her as an artist and spoke of her as a 'perfect German woman' – a label she found it impossible to live up to at the time and to live down ever since. Over the years he became relaxed in her presence and, despite her later denials, it seems most likely that she did spend a lot of time with him not only in Berlin but also in the more convivial and relaxed setting of his mountain retreat at Berchtesgaden. However, there is no reliable evidence that Riefenstahl ever became Hitler's mistress; and if Hanfstängl is to be believed, Hitler rejected her sexual approaches if she ever made any. It seems almost certain that they were never lovers.

After the war Riefenstahl repeatedly claimed that she was 'not interested in politics'. But she was interrogated by both the French and the American authorities and was in prison intermittently until 1948. Finally, it was decided not to prosecute her, and indeed no film-maker from the Nazi period was ever prosecuted as a war criminal. However, it is clear that from 1932 Riefenstahl enjoyed an access to Hitler that was shared by no other film-maker and that she could and did take any issue that concerned her direct to the Führer. This allowed Riefenstahl's talent to emerge in a unique way within the Third Reich.

Soon after taking power, Hitler appointed Joseph Goebbels as head of the Reich Film Association (Reichsfilmkammer). Riefenstahl became a member of this Association in 1934. Only members of the different branches of the Association (producers, directors, writers, cameramen, etc.) were allowed to work in the German film industry. All manuscripts and scenarios for production had to be approved, and without authorisation from the Association it was impossible to produce films. All Jews were excluded, as was anyone thought to be hostile to the regime. Although most films during the Third Reich were not overtly concerned with politics, censorship and control of the cinema was a cornerstone of the Nazi propaganda effort.[7] Goebbels and Hitler were keen film enthusiasts, and from the beginning the role of the cinema in influencing and forming public opinion was emphasised. 'We are convinced,' Goebbels wrote, 'that films constitute one of the most modern and scientific means of influencing the mass. Therefore a government must not neglect them.' By 1934, 14,000 people were employed in the myriad state and Party bodies concerned with control of the cinema industry. In 1935 the Reich invested over forty million Reichsmarks in theatre and cinema productions. Few regimes in history have curtailed and controlled artistic freedom so totally and yet so effectively used the cinema as a weapon of propaganda.

In the summer after he came to power Hitler summoned Riefenstahl. He instructed her to make a record of the annual Nazi Party rally in Nuremberg. According to Riefenstahl, she had only a few days to prepare. With whatever technicians and facilities she could muster she began shooting. During production she suffered what she regarded as appalling bureaucratic harassment from officials of the Propaganda Ministry. Apparently Goebbels was resentful at being by-passed and was determined to make Riefenstahl's life difficult. He seems to have succeeded. Riefenstahl later said that after the film was completed she collapsed and spent two months in hospital as a consequence of the strain.[8] This episode marks the beginning of what was to become a major feud between Goebbels and Riefenstahl which was to affect in one way or another all her further work during the Nazi period. It might explain why, after *Olympia*, she produced no other propaganda films for the Reich. On this occasion, as on many later encounters, Goebbels seems to have been upset that the person he wanted to make the film had been overlooked and Riefenstahl had been appointed over his head.

The one-hour film of the 1933 Nazi rally was called *Sieg des Glaubens* (*Victory of Faith*). It was funded directly by the Nazis and according to Party estimates was seen by at least twenty million Germans. It was apparently highly regarded at the time but was thought to be lost for many years until a print was recently discovered in Munich. The film is far more sophisticated and lavish than Riefenstahl describes it. The main reason for its disappearance was that it strongly featured, alongside Hitler, Ernst Röhm, the leader of the Sturmabteilung or the SA. The paramilitary 'Brownshirts' of the SA had played a central role in the rise to power of the Nazis, and Röhm and Hitler were very close. But this was to be Röhm's last moment of glory. It soon became clear to Hitler that Röhm and the two and a half million members of the SA presented a rival power faction to himself and a threat to the Nazi Party. In the 'Blood Purge' of June 1934 Hitler had Röhm and his leading associates murdered. Henceforth, their role in the history of the Nazi Party was to be written out. Riefenstahl's dramatic film became an embarrassment. It was withdrawn and not referred to again.[9] For Riefenstahl, *Victory of Faith* was a dress rehearsal for her biggest challenge yet, which came at the 1934 Nazi Party rally in Nuremberg.

Hitler was apparently delighted with *Victory of Faith* and asked Riefenstahl to direct a bigger and more ambitious film about the 1934 rally. This event was to be of supreme importance to the regime. After the bloody and violent events of June and the murders of Röhm and his closest supporters, it was vital to cover over any scars that might have been left in the Party. Furthermore, in August, Hindenburg died and Hitler proclaimed himself President and head of the armed forces. The Party rally later that year was to be the supreme expression of the unity of the Party behind the Führer, Adolf Hitler. Nothing was to be spared to help create the desired effect. The rally arena outside Nuremberg was extended. Albert Speer was called in to stage-manage the event and created some extraordinary effects. The rally would be experienced by three-quarters of a million visitors. In this context the film of the rally was of great importance in transmitting the message of unity behind the leader to millions more both in Germany and abroad.

Initially, Riefenstahl declined the offer to produce the film and suggested that Walter Ruttmann make it instead. But the film was too important and Hitler was convinced of Riefenstahl's film-making genius. He persuaded (or ordered) her to make the film and offered her whatever resources she needed. Riefenstahl finally accepted. It was extraordinary that a non-Party member, and a woman at that, should be allowed to film the holiest of holy rituals of the Nazi Party. From Hitler, Riefenstahl established her independence to work freely from the

Hitler and Leni Riefenstahl during filming of *Triumph des Willens*

control of Goebbels's Ministry and his battalions of officials, and doubtless all this contributed to the continuing tension between her and Goebbels. But ultimately, of course, all her 'independence' only came as a consequence of Hitler's respect for her and her direct line to the Führer. This was not independence in any sense we would understand it today. One mistake, one offence to the all-powerful Führer, and Riefenstahl would find herself, at best, in a concentration camp like the thousands of others who had dared to cross the Nazi leadership.

Riefenstahl set to work with a team of 135 technicians, drivers, officials and police guards led by sixteen prominent cameramen using thirty cameras. Bridges and towers were built and tracks were laid for the cameras to move along. An enormous flagpole was equipped with an electric lift to take the cameraman to the top as the marchers fanned out below. A fire engine was requisitioned to enable a camera at the top of a 90-foot ladder to film across the city rooftops. A ramp was built in the main square to allow the camera to track along with the marching troops. An airplane and an airship were put at Riefenstahl's disposal. In a frantic whirlwind of activity Riefenstahl, then thirty-two years old, organised her teams of cameramen and sound recordists and gave them all precise instructions as to what she required.[10]

The resulting film, *Triumph des Willens* (*Triumph of the Will*), has been called 'one of the greatest achievements, perhaps the most brilliant of all in the history of film propaganda'.[11] It is certainly an extraordinary evocation of the fascist and the totalitarian spirit on film. Thousands of marching men, lines of Party members and officials are choreographed around the symbols and the rituals of the Party. Everything is dedicated to the worship of the leader. The masses are there simply to create a vast human theatre in which the Party leaders can speak. And everything builds up to the climax of the Führer's address, timed for sunset. Hitler rants and raves against a spectacular backdrop in which a column of searchlights light up the sky. The music, the rituals, the flags, the masses are all defined in terms of their relationship to the will of the Führer. Everything is disciplined around strict obedience to the word of Hitler. The party is unified, the nation is one, the leader rules. Although the stage-management of the event was itself spectacular, Riefenstahl does more than simply record the rally for posterity. She uses all her skills as a film-maker to adulate the Party and worship the Führer. There is no doubt that while the film is a triumph of the cinema it is also one of the most fascistic films ever made.

Triumph of the Will has been analysed many times.[12] However, there are several points of relevance to *Olympia*. The opening of *Triumph of the Will* acts as a Prologue to set the scene for the rally and to a degree anticipates the Prologue of *Olympia*. Out of swirling clouds a plane appears. Hitler is seen looking out of the window of the plane over the city of Nuremberg. The plane lands. The deity arrives to inspect the host parading before him. The city of Nuremberg emerges from the mist. The city had been chosen by the Nazis because it so perfectly represented the Germanic spirit, and here we see Germany awakening from the Middle Ages, from the Renaissance and from the centuries that had led up to this moment. People come out and watch as Hitler passes by. From the start Hitler is presented as godlike, and Riefenstahl creates in the film the sense of a new dawn brought about by the Führer.

On the soundtrack, Wagner's *Meistersingers* slowly mixes into a version by Herbert Windt of the Nazi marching song, the 'Horst Wessel Lied'. Windt was probably the finest German film music composer of

Triumph des Willens

the time. He had been a serious classical composer before coming to the cinema; his opera *Andromache* had been premiered by the Berlin State Opera in 1932. Throughout *Triumph of the Will*, his Wagneresque music alternates with the oompah of traditional Nazi marching songs. This creates on the commentary-free soundtrack an effect almost as powerful as the pictures themselves. Windt became a close associate of Riefenstahl and was a natural choice when it came to choosing a composer for the music for *Olympia*.

Riefenstahl learnt a great deal from the experience of making *Triumph of the Will*. She successfully assembled and supervised a small army of brilliant and creative technicians. She asserted control over an event and succeeded in creating the effects she wanted her camera to capture within that event. She worked independently from the Ministry of Propaganda and Goebbels's officials, and she financed the film entirely from a distribution deal she negotiated with UFA, the giant production and distribution company. She was left to edit the film in her own time and in her own style. As with *Olympia*, Riefenstahl required a spectacle of vast proportions to start with in order to be able to mould her cinematic vision, but she was no mere chronicler of the event. Her film entered the spirit of the Nazi rally and created a supreme instrument of propaganda.[13]

When *Triumph of the Will* was released in March 1935 it was an instant success. The Nazis decided it was their most effective propaganda achievement yet. Abroad, it was well received. The film won the most prestigious award at that year's Venice Film Festival and, more surprisingly, it was awarded a special diploma at the Paris International Exposition. Hitler was delighted. Even Goebbels had to admit that the film had scored a gigantic triumph. There was no question that the most celebrated film-maker in Germany in the summer of 1935 was Leni Riefenstahl. She was young and glamorous, a dancer who had become a film star and had now turned film-maker. She was a confidante of the Führer himself. It looked as though she could do anything she wanted.

III

·························

PRODUCTION AND FINANCE

In analysing *Olympia* it is crucial to understand how and why the film was made and how its production fitted into the overall use that was made of the Games by the Nazis. Predictably there are several different versions of how *Olympia* came to be produced. Riefenstahl has said different things over the years. After the war she said to US Army Intelligence that Hitler commissioned her personally to make the film.[14] However, more recently she claimed that she was asked to produce the film by Dr Carl Diem, the General Secretary of the Olympic Organising Committee, on behalf of the IOC. In her memoirs, Riefenstahl claims that she was approached by Diem in the summer of 1935. Praising her as a great artist for the production of *Triumph of the Will*, Diem asked her to produce a film that would capture the spirit of the Olympics.[15]

Riefenstahl claims that she initially refused, having sworn never to make another documentary. She also claims to have been concerned about running up against Goebbels once more. However, over a period of time, Diem persuaded her to change her mind. He said that in the Olympic stadium the IOC and the Organising Committee would be in charge and it was they who were approaching Riefenstahl, not the Ministry for Propaganda and Enlightenment. Riefenstahl was persuaded, and began to think about the challenge of making a unified film out of the dozens of separate Olympic events. Slowly the form of the prologue began to take shape in her mind. According to Riefenstahl's own accounts, she went herself to UFA, who had distributed *Triumph of the Will*, and asked for the independent finance necessary to produce an extended film about the Games. They were sceptical. There had never been a successful feature-length film about the Games. Moreover, Riefenstahl wanted a year to edit the film. Surely, they asked, all interest in the Games would have faded by that time? They suggested weaving a love story in and out of the Games. Riefenstahl gave up and tried their competitors, Tobis or Tobisfilm. Friedrich Mainz, the head of the company, shared her vision of the film. He accepted that it would be in two parts and only completed long after the Games. They agreed on a budget of one and a half million

Reichsmarks, which Riefenstahl admits was a 'sensational commission, unheard of in Germany'.[16]

According to Riefenstahl, Goebbels soon heard of the commission and called her to the Ministry. He regarded her idea as a 'joke', saying that 'Filming the Games is only of use if the film can be shown a couple of days after they have ended.' Again, however, in her own account Riefenstahl claims she persisted. She insisted that she did not want to make newsreels but an artistic interpretation of the Games. Finally, after a second meeting, she got the tacit support of Goebbels. After several months of negotiations, Riefenstahl says, it was put to her that she should form her own independent production company to make the film, and in December 1935 she formed a limited company called Olympiade-Film GmbH of which she and her brother Heinz were the two directors. Riefenstahl says that to 'avoid high taxes' she was advised to transfer her shares in Olympiade-Film GmbH to the Propaganda Ministry free of charge, 'purely [as] a formality for tax purposes'. Partly under the control of the Film Credit Bank, a bank administered by the Propaganda Ministry for the making of feature films, Riefenstahl says she felt herself slowly being pulled under the influence of Goebbels's Propaganda Ministry, who were 'trying to exert more and more control over me'.

Just after Christmas 1935, Riefenstahl recounts, she met Hitler at his mountain lair at Berchtesgaden. She says he knew nothing of her plans but was delighted to be told that she was going to make a film about the Olympics. Hitler told her to have more confidence in herself and that she was the only person in Germany who could make a film about the Games. Apparently, Hitler assured Riefenstahl that she would have no problems with Goebbels because the IOC were organising the Games and Germany would simply be the hosts. He then confided to her that he had lost interest in the Games altogether because he feared the American blacks would take most of the medals and he did not want to see this. He ended by reassuring her that she would 'doubtless make a beautiful film'.

This account of the negotiations that led up to Riefenstahl's commission to produce the Olympic films is interesting, but it does not conform to the evidence that has since been found in Germany and is available in the Bundesarchiv in Koblenz. In order to understand the significance of this material, it's necessary to take the story back a stage.

Berlin was awarded the Games of 1936 by the International Olympic Committee at its Session in Barcelona in 1931. The only other candidate city, Barcelona itself, which had just hosted a World Exposition and built a new stadium, lost by 43 votes to 16 and had to wait sixty years for its chance to host the Games. Germany was still a democracy at the time, and the Organising Committee for the Games was presided over by Dr Theodor Lewald, the German IOC member. The Secretary of the Committee was Dr Carl Diem, the famous scholar, athlete and pioneer of physical education in Germany. Diem had led several German Olympic teams and had been in charge of the plans for the 1916 Berlin Games, cancelled because of the war. Both Diem and Lewald were interested in film and had been involved in the production of sports films. According to Olympic protocol, the Organising Committee was supposed to be a politically independent body responsible not to the government of the host country but to the International Olympic Committee based in Switzerland.

When Hitler came to power in 1933 a clash between the new Reichsministry for Sport – led by Hans von Tschammer und Osten, a close friend of Hitler – and the Organising Committee from the pre-Nazi era was inevitable. The new government created an Olympic Commission which was packed with Nazi sympathisers. In October 1933, Hitler reviewed preparations for the Games and took the crucial decision to expand the Games. This was to be the turning point in the preparations of the Berlin Olympics. Hitler authorised plans to extend the building of the stadium to seat 100,000 spectators, to build a new swimming stadium that would seat 18,000, and to construct a vast new sports complex to the north of Berlin called the Sports Forum. Hitler himself was unhappy with the architectural design of the main stadium and asked Albert Speer to come up with some ideas. Overnight, Speer produced a set of drawings showing how the steel skeleton already built in neo-classical style could be clad in a marble-like stone called travertine. The structure was to be reinforced with enormous cornices. This seemed far more in keeping with the image the Nazis wanted to portray in their architecture. Hitler agreed. The Nazis were later to claim that the Olympic Stadium was the first great building of the National Socialist regime.

It was decided that the Reich would finance this ambitious building programme. With the purse strings controlled by the pro-Nazi Olympic Commission, the power of the Olympic Organising Committee was drastically diminished. A period of tension ensued between these two bodies, both of which claimed to be organising the Games. But by the end of 1934 the Nazis had seized effective control over all the decision-making about the running of the Games, although Lewald and Diem still represented the Games to the IOC and to the outside world.

It's clear that it was decided at the highest level in the Reich, probably by Hitler himself, that the Games should be used as an opportunity to promote the achievements of Nazi Germany before the world. Hitler decided that money would be no problem in creating a national spectacle to show off Germany to the world via the thousands of journalists and the hundreds of thousands of visitors who were expected. It was decided that the Games would be the best ever, far exceeding the Los Angeles Games in scale and spectacle. The entire sports and military establishments were put to work. The Olympic Village, for instance, was constructed as 160 separate buildings each housing about twenty-five athletes. There were thirty-eight dining halls, a new 400-metre training track and an artificial lake set amid natural woodlands. It was to be many Olympics before the facilities on offer in Berlin were equalled for both participants and spectators.

Although the Nazis wanted to promote the orderliness and efficiency of the regime, they could not disguise the brutal facts of their rule. All political parties except the National Socialists were banned. Free trade unions were abolished. The press and other media were taken over by the Propaganda Ministry. From the beginning the Nazis began to put into effect the threats they had been making against the Jews. Laws segregating Jews from non-Jews were soon in operation. Jewish shops and businesses were marked out and attacked. The first phase of the Nazi persecution of the Jews culminated in the Nuremberg Laws of September 1935, which deprived Jews of German citizenship and all civil rights. Marriage between Jews and non-Jews was forbidden. In the face of this state anti-semitism there were many protests about holding the Games in Berlin. In America there was a coordinated campaign to remove the Games from Germany. The powerful

American Athletic Union called for a boycott. Avery Brundage (later President of the International Olympic Committee from 1952 to 1972) visited Berlin in 1934 on behalf of the US Olympic Committee on a fact-finding mission. His influential report recommended participation in the Games. In the public row that erupted in the United States, Brundage and his supporters finally won the day and the US Olympic Committee agreed to attend the Games.

This attitude towards the Games alarmed the Nazis, and they decided to back-pedal on the policy against the Jews. Anti-semitic banners were taken down. The city was cleaned up. Some Jews were even allowed to compete in the German team: Helen Mayer, a Jewish fencer, went on to win a silver medal. It was decided to allow American blacks to compete without an outcry even if this went against the grain of Nazi dogma on racial superiority. The Games were clearly of great importance to the Nazis as an instrument of propaganda. The idea of an official film of the Games fitted in with this overall perspective. Whoever made the film would have to accept the propagandist role that it would play. Whatever artistic ambitions Riefenstahl had for the film, it had behind it a clear political purpose.

In this context it is very unlikely that Diem would have approached Riefenstahl with a request to make a film of the Games without the support of the Olympic Commission and the Nazi leadership. Most probably Hitler knew about or even suggested the approach in the first place. Maybe Diem was deputed to approach Riefenstahl, and when she refused the offer to make the film Hitler asked her directly. Whatever Riefenstahl felt, she could not refuse *this* request. In August 1935 Hitler appointed Riefenstahl to direct the film.[17]

Despite her later claims, the evidence is that at first Riefenstahl worked closely and cordially with Goebbels. Goebbels's diaries reveal some of the negotiations that went on through the autumn of 1935. On 17 August, Goebbels wrote, 'Frl. Riefenstahl reported on the preparations for the Olympic film. She is a clever thing!' On 21 August funding for the project was approved by Hitler himself. Goebbels wrote: 'Monday: to the Führer. Conference ... For the Olympic film one and a half million [Reichsmarks] granted.' On 5 October he recorded: 'Discussed thoroughly her Olympic film with Leni

Riefenstahl. A woman who knows what she wants.'[18] On 13 October a contract with Riefenstahl was worked out. Goebbels wrote that he was very happy with it. The contract, between the Reichsminister for People's Enlightenment and Propaganda and Riefenstahl, is very simple.[19] It says that Riefenstahl 'will direct the overall administration and production of this film'. It confirms the budget of one and a half million Reichsmarks and includes a cash flow. It records that Riefenstahl herself will receive a personal remuneration of 250,000 Reichsmarks. Her only other duty is to keep and submit substantiated accounts of the budget. (Apparently she was opposed to this.) Her exclusive responsibility for the 'artistic creation and the organisational execution of the Olympic film' is reiterated. Finally the contract confirms that the German newsreel companies will subordinate themselves to Riefenstahl during the Games.

The contract is extraordinarily brief and vague for such a major undertaking. And Riefenstahl is given a remarkable degree of independence. Issues like property rights are not mentioned. Was the film ultimately the property of the Ministry of Propaganda, the government, or Riefenstahl? Who would benefit from the exploitation of the film? These questions were much later to cause some controversy. Furthermore, the IOC, who in theory control all rights in the Olympic Games and all exploitation of the Games, are not a party to the contract or even mentioned in it. This contract more than anything else shows that the Nazi state had effectively taken over the Games and that Riefenstahl's commission came directly from the Reich and not through any intermediary like the IOC.

In November 1935 Riefenstahl established her independent production company to produce the film, Olympiade-Film GmbH, and a further contract was signed with the newsreel companies. Goebbels knew that the financing of the film would be critical. A loose contract could work in his favour, despite Riefenstahl's independence, if he controlled the funding. Riefenstahl claimed that the finance for the film came entirely through the distribution deal with Tobis. But documents in the Bundesarchiv reveal conclusively that although Riefenstahl got a distribution deal with Tobis the actual funding for the film came entirely from the Propaganda Ministry. There can be no doubt that *Olympia*, like every other film made in Germany at this time, was part of the overall film output controlled by the Ministry of Propaganda.

But Riefenstahl had insisted on and had won a measure of independence that was to be crucial in the making of the film. She had laid down conditions on which she would be willing to work; and she had her 'hot line' to Hitler, which she used frequently. Her memoirs recount four separate meetings with Hitler during the pre-production period. At each one she came away with what she wanted. This, too, in its curious way added to her independence. As long as she understood the role that film was to play in promoting the Games and the Reich, then she could operate independently of the Propaganda Ministry. To a modern film-maker this might not seem much like real independence. To a film-maker operating in Nazi Germany it was considerable.

IV
. . . .
SETTING UP

In the late autumn of 1935 Riefenstahl began her preparations for *Olympia*. Walter Traut was appointed Production Manager. Traut had been one of the group around Dr Fanck who made the mountain films and was a close friend of Riefenstahl, having managed both *The Blue Light*, and *Triumph of the Will*. In the massive logistical enterprise of organising crews, equipment, film stock and processing, travel and subsistence, Traut was to play a central role. Working for Traut were three assistant production managers: Konstantin Boenisch, with responsibility for all tracks, dollies, cranes, ladders, etc; Arthur Kiekebusch, with responsibility for all cameras and lenses; and Rudolf Fichtner, responsible for filming outside Berlin. So complex did the operation become that some of these assistant production managers themselves had a further ten assistants working for them during the course of the Games. Also important at senior managerial level was Walter Grosskopf, the financial or business manager of the film. Both Traut and Grosskopf were also officers of Riefenstahl's company, Olympiade-Film.[20]

The production offices, known as the Haus Ruhwald, were located in a castle in the Spandauer Berg in west Berlin. From here all the main venues were only a few minutes' travel away. The entire crew

would live here before and during the Games. A hundred and twenty beds were brought in and the cafeteria acquired a reputation for the quality of its breakfasts – Riefenstahl doubtless understood that the way to win the hearts of a film crew was to feed them well. The offices contained four large cutting rooms, all rigged out with the latest editing desks, a preview theatre, a darkroom and a small printing room, a lounge, a meeting room and a variety of offices for the production team. Riefenstahl said they were 'sumptuously appointed'. Film vaults were built under the supervision of Johannes Häussler, who was given the job of ensuring that there was always a sufficient supply of film stock. It was estimated that about 400,000 metres of film would be shot which, after development and processing, then needed to be viewed and logged. This was roughly equivalent to three thousand cans of negatives and prints, all of which needed to be in the right place at the right time.

In the spring of 1936, Riefenstahl started to assemble her technical team.[21] She found that most of the top German feature-film cameramen were not available and many of the newsreel cameramen mounted an unofficial boycott, refusing to work for a woman. So she built up her own team, the nucleus of which were young, south German sportsmen, many of whom had worked in Fanck's group. Of this core team, four cameramen were to make a major contribution to *Olympia*.

Hans Ertl had been a mountaineer hired by Fanck to create special mountain effects like avalanches. Slowly he became fascinated by film and taught himself the principles of photography. In 1934 he filmed a German expedition to the Himalayas. Riefenstahl saw the film Ertl took and immediately asked him to join her. He worked on various Olympic preparation films in the run-up to *Olympia*. Riefenstahl describes Ertl as a 'workaholic' and as enormously ambitious, making himself unpopular because he wanted to shoot everything himself. One of his achievements was to build a camera encased in a box that could shoot above and below water. This was used with magnificent effect for the Diving events. Interestingly, the team preparing the television coverage for the Barcelona Olympic Games have produced a camera that can shoot above and below the water-line, and claimed this is as an 'Olympic first' – but Hans Ertl got there first over fifty years ago. In addition to the Swimming and Diving events, Ertl also took the magnificent panning shots of the Athletics events from specially constructed towers in the main stadium.

Walter Frentz was another self-made cameraman who produced his own 16 mm films about kayak racing before being spotted by the industry and offered work at UFA. From 1931, Frentz shot many UFA films but always excelled at those which dealt with water sports. In 1933 he worked for Riefenstahl on *Victory of Faith*, and in the following year he worked with her again on *Triumph of the Will*. Here he had his own triumph by photographing the close-ups of Hitler as he travelled by car through Nuremberg. A German film magazine said this footage was 'so thrilling it was as if Frentz had caught the current of life instead of celluloid and forced it in his camera.'[22] (Frentz later became Hitler's personal cameraman.) He produced some of the misty, romantic scenes in the Olympic Village, and also shot the Yachting events at Kiel and the marathon in Berlin.

Gustav 'Guzzi' Lantschner was another from the Fanck school. As an expert skier he had acted in several of the mountain films, including *Storms over Mont Blanc* with Riefenstahl in 1930. He later claimed to be Riefenstahl's lover for a short time. In 1929 Lantschner joined the Nazi Party and became an active propagandist for the Party cause in southern Germany. He worked with Riefenstahl on *Triumph of the Will* and on another short Party film about the German army, in 1935. At the Winter Olympics held at Garmisch-Partenkirchen in the German Alps in 1936 he won a silver medal for downhill skiing. For *Olympia*, Lantschner would shoot the Diving, Gymnastics and Equestrian events.

Heinz von Jaworsky was yet another who had worked with Fanck and Riefenstahl on the mountain films of the early 1930s. Working his way up, he eventually became assistant cameraman to Hans Schneeberger and then Ernst Udet. He refused an offer to work on *Triumph of the Will*, saying it was too political, although he later went on to shoot several wartime propaganda documentaries and feature films. On *Olympia* he specialised in the use of the Kinamo camera, which held only five metres of film and was small enough to be used unobtrusively. A lot of the crowd cutaways were shot this way and Jaworsky's footage adds a unique element to the film.

These four, relatively inexperienced cameramen were closest to

Riefenstahl during the planning and shooting of *Olympia*. She preferred working with them as she felt they were more willing to try out new ideas. Riefenstahl repeatedly said that the more experienced feature-film cameramen were too conventional for her. But there were several other cinematographers who were to play an important role in the making of the film. At the other end of the scale from Jaworsky's miniature Kinamo camera were the giant telescopic lenses used by Hans Scheib. To shoot the Berlin Games, Scheib acquired an enormous 600 mm lens, the longest telephoto lens then available. Riefenstahl wanted to use this camera to capture the emotion on the faces of the athletes. The camera could be placed well away from the action so as not to intrude but still catch expressions of pain and anxiety, of triumph and elation, giving the film a particularly human edge. The lens was also used to capture scenes within the crowd, faces watching and moments of joy and disappointment. However, there was one problem. The 600 mm lens was very slow and with the film stocks in use could usually only guarantee an exposure when the aperture was fully open and there was bright light available. Unfortunately, the first few days of the Games were overcast and gloomy and it rained frequently. In these lighting conditions Scheib could not get an exposure and several moments that he and Riefenstahl had planned to film were missed. The lens came into its own in the second half of the first week, when the weather improved, capturing some memorable moments in the Athletics competition.

Kurt Neubert was one of the best known slow-motion experts in Europe. He, too, had shot sequences for the Fanck mountain films and had known Riefenstahl for some years. She was so keen to employ his skills in the film that she booked him nearly a year in advance. Neubert used giant DeBrie cameras that ran film through the gate at up to 96 frames per second (four times as fast as for real-time photography). The footage shot by Neubert and his colleague Eberhard von der Heyden is some of the most stunning in the film.

From May onwards, Riefenstahl and her team began the process of detailed planning. Riefenstahl worked on what she called her 'Manuscript', which was a set of notes, sketches and observations in which she developed her core ideas. Her cameramen worked on various devices for capturing the action. It was clear that many good shots

Hans Scheib in the main stadium with the longest telephoto lens available in 1936

could be taken from the inner field of the main stadium, and yet it was difficult to move here without distracting the athletes. After months of negotiating with different officials, Riefenstahl finally got permission to build two steel towers in the infield. These enabled the cameramen to take good all-round panning shots and, with the telephoto lenses, some of the big close-ups Riefenstahl wanted. But wherever the cameras were put they seemed to block someone's view and provide new objections. Eventually permission was also given to dig pits around the· high jump and the long jump and at the end of the 100 metres sprint track. From these the cameramen could gain good low-angle images of the competitors without distracting anyone. Officials of both the International Olympic Committee and the International Amateur Athletics Federation were concerned about these pits and some of them had to be filled in and moved at the last minute. The pit at the end of the 100 metres track proved too close for comfort, and in one of the heats shown in the final film Jessie Owens can be seen nearly running into it. The officials were furious and made the production team remove all

the pits from around the track. Only the pits for the jumping events remained.

Hans Ertl developed a system to film the 100 metres. A camera, without an operator, was catapulted along steel tracks down the side of the running track at the same speed as the sprinters and slightly ahead of them looking back on the front runners. This was tried out at the German National Athletics Championships in the spring before the Games and after some experimentation worked well. Three days before the start of the Games the International Amateur Athletics Federation (IAAF) ruled that the catapult mechanism

Riefenstahl and her team prepare for a long
tracking shot on the field outside the main stadium

would distract the sprinters and the whole device had to be dismantled.[23]

Other techniques were developed to get new and original angles on events. A scaffolding platform a hundred metres long was constructed at the rowing course at Grünau. A camera on tracks was pulled along by a car to follow the final dramatic sprint of the rowers. The camera team also borrowed a small airship from the Luftwaffe to film the rowing from the air. Minutes before the competitions were due to start, Riefenstahl was forbidden to use the airship in case of an accident. She was furious but could do nothing. Small cameras were tied to balloons and let off over the action, but none of the footage shot this way was steady enough to use.

In May, Walter Frentz was sent to Kiel to prepare for the yachting events. He received excellent co-operation from the organisers and soon began to send back some brilliant photography. Most of the footage used in the final film that was shot from the boats themselves was taken by Frentz during training as no cameras were allowed on the boats during the actual races. The idea of using training footage soon spread to the other sports as the camera teams struggled to find ways round the restrictions imposed on them. At Grünau, Jaworsky sat in on some of the boats during practices, filming the rowing team from the cox's point of view. At the swimming pool, Hans Ertl took close-ups of swimmers during training from a rubber dinghy. Cameras were put on the saddles of horses. Frentz even fixed tiny cameras to marathon runners in training to film their feet running. Much of the material shot in June and July before the Games began was used in the final version of *Olympia*.

In June, Riefenstahl hired Willy Zielke to shoot the Prologue. Zielke was a remarkably talented individual, at this time under the influence of the surrealist movement. He was imprisoned in an asylum when Riefenstahl secured his release and sent him to Greece to start shooting the background material that would be needed. At the Acropolis, he produced superb effects with the use of smoke powder to give a haze over his shots. With this and the use of soft focus, he created an atmospheric sense of dreamlike mystery.

As the opening of the Games drew near, Riefenstahl took on more and more technicians with the specific skills needed to complete her vision. Leo de Laforgue was employed to take the close-up shots of

Hitler and other VIPs. Helmuth von Stwolinski came in to shoot some of the rowing events at Grünau, and Wilhelm Siem worked with Frentz on the sailing events at Kiel. Fritz von Friedl was brought in as a tracking-shot specialist and was set to work at the swimming pool. Hasso Hartnagel joined the team as a well-known crane shot expert, and Andor von Barsy took the shots around Berlin. Dr Walter Hege, an expert on ancient Greece, assisted the filming in Greece. During the Games he shot from the roof of the stadium with his female camera assistant, the Baroness Ursula von Loewenstein. Soon the list of cameramen and advisors read like a Who's Who of the German cinema industry.

Apart from the cameras used at fixed locations and for slow-motion effects, which were heavy and cumbersome, Riefenstahl favoured lighter, mobile cameras wherever possible. Her cameramen used Sinclairs along with Bell and Howell cameras. They also used the new Askania shoulder-camera which held a magazine of 60 metres of film, enough for about two minutes of shooting. The achievement of *Olympia* is all the more remarkable when one considers the technical limitations of these cameras. The Arriflex was not introduced until the late 1930s. One of the most lightweight and reliable cameras available, its use by German cameramen during the war gave them an inestimable propaganda advantage over the Allies. The Arriflex is still one of the most reliable, all-purpose film cameras in use today. Yet Riefenstahl had none of the advantages of its use. The cameras she was using were still relatively heavy, difficult to operate and slow to use.

Some of the larger cameras used in Berlin also made a terrible racket as the film was pulled through the camera mechanism. This would have put off the athletes and so special housings or 'blimps' were constructed to sound-proof the cameras. Guzzi Lantschner constructed a leather blimp for his camera for use in the stadium pits very near where the athletes would compete. Finally, it is worth noting that *Olympia* was made before the zoom lens was introduced. Within a few years of the Berlin Games, zoom lenses of sufficient quality for cinema use began to appear. Again, none were available to Riefenstahl and her team. So much that is now taken as standard in the world of sports cinematography was still in the future in 1936.

Simultaneously with the camera testing went trials with different types of film stock. In 1936 there were three main types of film stock available – Kodak, Agfa, and Perutz stock, which was hardly ever used for feature films. The average film speeds were equivalent to 20–32 ASA, then considered fast.[24] Tests were carried out on faces and people, on architecture and stadia and on landscapes with green, grassy backgrounds. To everyone's surprise the shots of people looked best on Kodak, since it gave the best halftones; buildings and architecture looked at their most real on Agfa, and the Perutz stock responded well to shots with a lot of green in them. So it was decided to use all three stocks and for a cameraman to be issued with the stock most appropriate for that day's filming. This meant that Johannes Häussler had not only to ensure that enough film was always available, but that there was always enough of each type of stock when needed.

Once shot, the film was taken to the Geyer laboratories for processing. Riefenstahl got Geyer to agree that every frame of film sent in for processing would be returned on the following day. It was crucial for the production team to see what was being shot. If there were any problems, new instructions had to be given or, where possible, re-shoots arranged immediately. It was anticipated that about 15,000 metres (nearly 50,000 feet), equivalent to nearly ten hours of film, would be shot each day during the Games. To deal with such quantities, Geyer bought a new developing machine and two special cars were used to transport exposed film between the different venues and the laboratories. Two editors, Max Michel and Heinz Schwarzmann, viewed everything as soon as it had been processed and their written reports were passed back to the cameramen and to Riefenstahl.

In July, Riefenstahl led an expedition to Greece to join the team who were to film the lighting of the Olympic flame at Olympia and its journey to Athens. Dr Hege and Willy Zielke had already been shooting material in Greece, but during the few days of what amounted to Riefenstahl's 'state visit' very little usable new material was shot.

The Opening Ceremony of the Games took place on Saturday, 1 August. For the first time the Games were organised over a sixteen-day period and the Closing Ceremony took place on the evening of Sunday, 16 August.[25] The weather was bad for the first few days but gradually improved and was mostly fine for the second week. Every evening during the course of the Games, Riefenstahl called all her senior colleagues together for a production meeting. Laboratory reports of the film were analysed, faults were assessed and decisions made on how to rectify them. Johannes Häussler would review the amount of film stock being used. Walter Traut would assess the problems of the day's filming. Frequently, passes and armbands were not recognised by officials and the camera teams would be denied access to some important event. On one day, neither Riefenstahl nor any of the camera teams were admitted to the main stadium because of a misunderstanding. Every day there were disputes like this to be sorted out. Riefenstahl would brief each cameraman on the next day's work. Every sequence would be talked through, each event prepared for in detail. These production meetings often went on until the early hours of the morning.

Filming continued after the Games were over. Sequences were shot in the swimming and diving pools and some of the gymnasts who had won events were asked to come back to be filmed. Then, in September, Willy Zielke went off to a remote part of the Baltic coast near Danzig to film the rest of the Prologue. Filming was finally completed at the end of September.

With all the film 'in the can', the massive task of editing the mountain of rushes began. Some 250 hours of material had been shot. First, everything had to be logged so that material could be quickly found during the editing. Each sport or event was given a prefix and each subdivision of the sport was given an additional number. For instance, spectators were classed as prefix 10. Spectators in sunlight were classed as 10–1a; spectators in shadow were 10–1b; spectators applauding were 10–1c, and so on. The Modern Pentathlon was classed as prefix 70, the Pentathlon horse-riding was 70–20, the horse-riding at the water jump was 70–20c, etc. Logging the film took a month. Viewing the rushes took ten hours a day for more than two months.

During this stage Dr Goebbels struck once again. He had clearly decided that Riefenstahl was not up to the task of completing this mammoth project, and again he wanted to install a new director. He confronted Riefenstahl with a set of charges, claiming she had misbehaved on several occasions during the Games, especially by insulting sports officials, and that she had shown too much interest in the black American athletes. Goebbels wanted the glory of making the film to go to Hans Wiedemann, Vice-President of the Reich Film Chamber, the Party man who had made the film of the Winter Olympics in Garmisch and who had always been Goebbels's preferred candidate to make *Olympia*. He seemed to believe that the task of editing 400,000 metres of material was too much for a woman, and he suggested that Wiedemann should now replace Riefenstahl as director. Riefenstahl went straight to Goebbels, who records in his diary: 'September 18, 1936 (Friday); Ministry; Riefenstahl has complaints about Wiedemann. But she is badly hysterical. A further proof that women cannot master such assignments.'[26]

In October, Goebbels sent a team of accountants to the Olympiade-Film Company to carry out a surprise audit. They reported countless examples of excess and also what on the surface appeared to be financial theft. The mismanagement of the accounts by Grosskopf seemed to be on such a scale as to be more than just incompetence. Company property had apparently been sold at great discount or given away to Riefenstahl's favourites. Documents and records were not in place. Items had been acquired and then not used. Receipts had not been issued for advances. Goebbels insisted that the company should in future be subject to a strict monthly cost-reporting procedure to the Ministry which had financed the whole venture.

Unperturbed, Riefenstahl responded by demanding another 500,000 Reichsmarks in order to finish the project. Having viewed most of the footage, she had now decided that it was necessary to edit two films out of the material. Again, after meeting her, Goebbels wrote in his diary: 'November 6, 1936; Fräulein Riefenstahl demonstrates her hysteria to me. It is impossible to work with this wild woman. Now she wants half a million more for her film and to make two out of it. Yet it stinks to high heaven in her shop. I am cool right down to my heart. She cries. That is the last weapon of women. But that does not work on me any more. She should work and keep order.'[27]

Goebbels and Riefenstahl had by this point come to a complete impasse. Riefenstahl resorted to her old trick of referring directly to Hitler. It took some weeks to arrange a meeting, but finally they met in December after Hitler's adjutant had personally intervened. Riefenstahl claims that at the beginning Hitler was on Goebbels's side, having already heard his version of the story, but slowly she talked him round.

Hitler said she would receive a decision in a few days. It is not known what went on between Hitler and Goebbels, but a few days later Riefenstahl was told by Hitler's adjutant that a new arrangement had been struck with the Propaganda Ministry. She would receive her extra half-million marks and she would not in future be disturbed by the Ministry. Once again Riefenstahl had played her trump card and had established her 'independence' from the film-making hierarchy of the Propaganda Ministry. But although Riefenstahl was now free to continue her work, Goebbels extracted his revenge on her collaborators. Friederich Mainz, the director of Tobis, who had originally helped her set up the project, was dismissed, as was Ernst Jäger, her Press Chief and ex-editor of the main German film magazine, *Film-Kurier*. Accused of having a Jewish wife, Jäger left Germany for the United States.

Finally, in January 1937, after preparing a detailed outline of the film, Riefenstahl was able to start work on the creative editing process. She threw herself into this task with extraordinary energy and worked virtually uninterrupted for a whole year on the editing. Three-quarters of the original film was discarded. Much of it was technically unusable; some of it dealt with events that were no longer to be included. The remaining 100,000 metres had to be cut down to 6,000 metres for the final film. Riefenstahl herself carried out the edit with a team of assistants. Her principal editing assistant was Erna Peters, who had been involved in *Olympia* from the beginning. Riefenstahl has always said how important it was to get the 'architecture' of the film right. Where does the film begin? Where does it end? What are its high points? What are the less dramatic events? In editing a documentary in which the director does not know during shooting how an event will turn out, it is essential to get this dramatic structure right. Most film-makers assemble a film first and then look for the rhythm and pacing to create the high and low points. Riefenstahl went the other way about it, and having given every sequence its place then worked on giving each event the pacing necessary to fit into the overall structure. She clearly saw the process of editing as being like that of composing music, and wrote about cutting the film 'like a symphony ... according to the laws of aesthetics and rhythm'.

Riefenstahl and her team worked for months, including weekends and holidays. She says they all became 'entranced' with the film. It took two months to edit the Prologue, and Riefenstahl got to the point where she nearly binned everything she had done and started again. It then took five months to edit Part One, but by this time she felt she had mastered the subject and Part Two was completed in two months. The timings were then sent to Herbert Windt, who started to write the music to accompany the film. Meanwhile Riefenstahl began the long process of mixing the sound. Most of the sound recorded during the Games proved to be unusable because it consisted of simply the roar of the crowd. With the exception of the short speech by Hitler opening the Games, everything else was post-synched. The feet of the runners, the breathing of the horses, the crash of the hammer and the discus, the sound of the wind in the sails, the cheering of the spectators, everything was recorded and mixed together in the studios in Berlin. This would have been a gigantic task using modern digital technology. With the technology available in 1936 – optical sound tracks on film negative stock – the difficulties were awesome. There was no 'rock and roll' facility by which it is possible to stop and start any number of times, inserting or recording over previous tracks, as with modern mixing desks. Each optical reel of negative film – about ten minutes of running time – had to be recorded and mixed in real time from start to finish. Then it had to be processed and a print made, which sometimes took a whole day, before it could be played back. A film-maker of today can only marvel at how such effects could be achieved when every sound had to be recorded and mixed in this way.

The sound mixing took six weeks with four separate dubbing mixers working full-time, to produce what today would be called the effects tracks. The commentary tracks were recorded with famous radio commentators providing the voice-over. In January 1938 the music was recorded. Riefenstahl was delighted with it, saying it made the film come alive; she hugged Herbert Windt when she heard it. The Berlin Philharmonic played the music, conducted by Windt himself. The final tracks were then taken to the most advanced dubbing suite in Germany, but still there were too many tracks to mix down and the result was a background hum which Riefenstahl described as sounding 'like a waterfall'. The audio engineers pronounced that nothing could be done. There were too many tracks and the mixing was too complex.

Riefenstahl yet again insisted. The engineers came up with a new set of filters to take away the hum and the work continued. Hermann Storr was the final dubbing mixer and he worked with Riefenstahl for two months, from twelve to fourteen hours a day. Riefenstahl has said that this was the most taxing part of making the film and on several occasions they felt they could not go on. But somehow they completed the task. The sound plays a crucial part in the final film and the mixing represents an extraordinary achievement in any setting, but a heroic one bearing in mind the primitive technology which Riefenstahl and her team had to operate with. Yet again Riefenstahl demonstrated that she would not take 'no' for an answer and somehow motivated her team to carry on to even greater heights to achieve what she wanted.

About early March 1938 the film was finished. After nearly three years of work with a team that at one point numbered almost three hundred, after eighteen months of post-production, after political arguments and personal rows, the 250 hours of shot material had been edited down to a two-part film of three and three-quarter hours. The truly Olympian effort of making the first major feature film of any Olympic Games had been completed. The film was ready to be seen.

V
....
THE PROLOGUE AND OPENING CEREMONY

Olympia begins with a stunning opening sequence. For twelve minutes the film evokes a classical past and celebrates the human form. The opening suggests the power and beauty of the human body in motion, themes which underlie the whole film. The camerawork shows the force of Riefenstahl's imagination and the genius of the team working with her, especially Willy Zielke. The photography provides a haunting set of images, setting the film in its epic proportions. The opening sequence tells us that *Olympia* will be much more than a documentary about a sporting event: it will affect us on a far more profound level.

The opening credits mention only two names. In the English version, Leni Riefenstahl is credited as producer and the other credit is for the music by Herbert Windt. In the original German version, the words used to describe Riefenstahl are not the conventional term for director, 'Regie', but 'Gesamtleitung und Künstlerische Gestaltung', or roughly 'under the leadership and artistic supervision of'. With the team Riefenstahl gathered round her to produce the film and with the amount of material shot, it is interesting that she should use this term to describe her role. Curiously there is no attempt to replicate this concept on foreign versions of the film, where she is credited not as the director but as the producer.[28]

The opening shots mix through swirling clouds to classical ruins. To the ponderous Wagnerian rhythms of Windt's music, the camera tracks across broken columns scattered over the ground and mixes to further ruins. With the camera still moving, the film dissolves to a long shot of a Greek temple arising out of the ruins. The camera tracks round this temple and finally the film mixes to a static wide shot of the Parthenon which fills the screen with its magnificence. Tracking past the Doric columns, the film dissolves to a series of close-ups of faces from Greek statues – Medusa, Aphrodite and Apollo. Then, with the camera on the move again, the film dissolves to wider shots of the statues of Aphrodite and the Faun and back to the heads of Achilles and Paris. One head is superimposed over another. Finally we arrive at the naked statue of Myron's discus thrower and, as the camera rotates past the statue, the film mixes to live action of an almost naked man who comes to life throwing the discus. After the slow rhythm of the images of classical antiquity, the music changes pace and the film erupts with a montage of low-angle images of men throwing the discus, putting the shot and throwing the javelin.

The pace slows again and the camera lingers on an image of the putting shot being tossed from one outstretched hand to another. There is then a slow mix to arms waving, like corn in the wind, in the same rhythm as the shot putter. Another mix reveals a naked female dancer, who moves at the same gentle pace as the arms in the wind. A montage of naked female dancers follows. There is a dancer with a hoop and then the slow arm-waving of dancers choreographed in what Riefenstahl called 'eurhythmics' ('Schwingen').[29] Over the last of these images a flame is superimposed, and as flames take over the screen the film mixes to the supposed kindling of the sacred flame at Olympia. It has been claimed that Riefenstahl herself appears as one of these nude dancers, but this seems unlikely and does not accord with either her

own later accounts of the shooting of the sequence or those of Zielke.

The overall effect of these opening minutes is to extol the power and the glory of classical antiquity and to hypnotise the viewer with the beauty and grace of human movement. Columns and temples, naked young athletes and dancers create a powerful and erotic opening sequence in which the viewer is drawn first into the culture and history which the Olympic movement invokes and then into the physical achievement which the film will go on to celebrate. The prologue was shot under the supervision of Willy Zielke, not in Greece but in the most distant part of eastern Germany, in an area near the Lithuanian border known as the Valley of Silence. The location was remote enough for him to work in seclusion, and the filming was done after the Games were over when the sun was already low in the skies, providing some dramatic backdrops and long shadows. The transition shot from the statue of the discus thrower of Myron to live action proved difficult. The solution again reveals the ingenuity which Riefenstahl and her team brought to the production. They persuaded Erwin Huber, the German decathlon champion, to take part in the filming because he was almost exactly the same size as the statue. He stood behind a glass screen in the same pose and the outline of the statue was painted in black on the glass. Using a mixture of artificial lighting and daylight, a transition was effected by which the statue appears to come to life and the film moves from the world of the classical imagination to the physical world of the athlete.

The Games of 1936 were the first to use the Torch Ceremony which has since become so much a part of Olympic ritual. The idea of kindling a 'sacred' flame in Olympia and running it to the site of the Games was the invention of Carl Diem, Secretary of the Berlin Organising Committee. This flame then lit the giant Olympic Torch in the stadium which burned throughout the Games and was extinguished at the end of the Closing Ceremony. It is perhaps not surprising that this piece of pyrotechnic pageantry should come out of Nazi Germany, but it has endured as one of the most potent symbols of the Games.

The sequence of the Olympic Torch ceremony again provided Riefenstahl's team with major problems. When she travelled to Greece in July 1936 to film the kindling of the flame, Riefenstahl was bitterly disappointed by what she found. The sacred *altis* at Olympia was obscured by cars and motorbikes. Even the Greek boy in his classical Greek dress who was to light the flame did not suit the atmosphere Riefenstahl had imagined. And finally on the day itself there was such commotion that it proved impossible to film the event through the crowds. Riefenstahl admits that in all the hubbub her team missed the crucial moment of the lighting of the flame. Most documentary film-makers will know the feeling! As the camera car moved to follow the torch-bearer it was stopped by a row of policemen. The official IOC stickers on the windscreen meant nothing to the local police and there was a delay of several vital minutes while the torch procession moved further away. It was only after Riefenstahl had burst into tears that the police allowed the camera convoy to proceed. Riefenstahl decided that it would be necessary to stage her own ceremony in order to achieve the effect she wanted.

A few kilometres from Olympia, Riefenstahl saw one of the torch-bearers, who had handed on the flame, resting in the shadow of a tree. This dark-haired boy of eighteen or nineteen was exactly what

Anatol, the Greek torch-bearer

Riefenstahl had been looking for. She stopped the car and the camera team tried to speak to him. He spoke no German and they could manage very little Greek, but somehow Riefenstahl persuaded the boy to come with them to restage the ceremony. His name was Anatol Dobriansky and in his way he became one of the stars of *Olympia*. Riefenstahl took him to Delphi, and the whole sequence of the lighting of the Olympic flame was reconstructed at the site of the temple of the sacred oracle – a location which had no connection with the original Olympic Games. Apparently, although reluctant at first, Anatol entered into the spirit of the filming and he was soon behaving like a precocious film star, refusing to run in certain ways and insisting on how his part should be played.

The sequence as staged by Riefenstahl creates a powerful effect. The camera uses star filters to give the flame a halo-like glow. A succession of runners carry the flame through the theatre and the temples at Delphi and across a dramatic landscape of mountain, wood and seashore. Briefly the film cuts from Riefenstahl's idealised vision of the ceremony back to shots of the actual event, with crowds lining the roadside cheering. Then there follows a sequence in which the camera tracks across a relief map of Europe following the four thousand mile route of the torch procession across Greece, through Bulgaria, Yugoslavia, Hungary, Austria and Czechoslovakia to Germany. Over the map a model of each capital city is superimposed along with its name. Sometimes a few frames of newsreel film are mixed in. A variety of mattes and superimpositions then bring up live action, fleeting glimpses of a runner with the torch and the flags of each nation. The composite effect would be a credit to most computer animation systems today, and yet it was created entirely out of 'opticals' made on the negative in the laboratory.

As the map reaches Germany and the flag of the Swastika fills the screen, the music reaches a crescendo with the fanfare theme most characteristic of Windt. Aerial shots of the spectacular stadium packed with 100,000 people (taken from a Zeppelin airship, the 'Hindenburg') are mixed with shots of the giant ten-ton Olympic bell cast specially for the occasion. Finally, thirteen minutes into the film, the music gives way to the sound of a cheering crowd. At last we are inside the stadium as thousands stand, their hands held out straight, in the *Sieg Heil* salute.

As the trumpets sound Windt's Olympic fanfare, the camera pans along the flags of all the nations and settles on the Olympic flags, fluttering in the wind.

For the Opening Ceremony, Riefenstahl had managed to position a total of thirty-six cameras around the stadium. The next few minutes of the film show the entry of the athletes into the stadium at the beginning of the day's ceremonies. It is only after the Greeks have entered the stadium that we see the first shot of Hitler, a wide shot of him in the enclosure reserved for the head of state and other VIPs, including Count Baillet-Latour, the President of the International Olympic Committee. Hitler salutes. The Swedish, British, Indian, Japanese and American teams march into the stadium. The first close-up of Hitler appears between the Austrian and the Italian teams. The French team, remarkably, raise their arms in the *Sieg Heil* salute as they march into the stadium. (They later claimed they were giving an Olympic salute, not the fascist salute!) Finally, in accordance with Olympic custom, the host nation enters. As always, the biggest cheer is for the home team.

Hitler at the Opening Ceremony

After the roar of the crowd all falls silent for Hitler, who proclaims the Games open. The fifteen words spoken by Hitler are the only part of the film recorded with synchronous sound. It is part of Olympic ritual that the head of state reads in his own language the words laid down in the Olympic Charter: 'I declare open the Games of Berlin celebrating the eleventh Olympiad of the modern era.' It is often claimed that Hitler abused this moment by making a political speech. As can be seen from the film, this is untrue. Hitler had probably never made such a short speech in his life, but the film faithfully records what happened.

Riefenstahl's cameramen had to have special clearance to operate near Hitler's enclosure. The cameras were much larger than usual since they were recording synch sound and were suspended on ropes a short distance from the VIP enclosure. Hitler had given Riefenstahl personal approval to film the opening speech and had agreed with her the exact location of the cameras. Because the moment could not be repeated, Riefenstahl wanted to use two cameras in case there was a technical fault. Minutes before Hitler was due to arrive in the stadium, two SS men began to remove the cameras. Riefenstahl shouted at them that Hitler himself had approved the camera positions and the cameras had to stay. The SS men explained that they had instructions from Goebbels to remove them. Riefenstahl refused to leave and the SS men went away. When Goebbels arrived he was apparently furious and screamed at Riefenstahl that she was trying to take over the whole show. But Riefenstahl prevailed. And the cameras remained. This brief moment is another illustration of Riefenstahl's extraordinary capacity to ensure that she got what she wanted. As always, her 'independence' was ultimately subject to Hitler's whim, but she still managed to get her way.

The film then dissolves to the Unter den Linden and to shots of the Olympic torch being carried down streets lined with cheering crowds held back by storm-troopers. To the sound of Windt's fanfare, there is then one of the finest shots in the history of Olympic film-making. The runner carries the torch through the short entrance-way into the stadium. Riefenstahl told her cameraman to set his exposure for the light conditions *inside* the stadium. The effect created is that the torch is run through a few moments of darkness into the light of the stadium. There, in almost religious splendour, the runner appears from the darkness and stands bathed in light, his back to the camera, holding the torch in his right hand. In front of him we see the stadium packed with people and all the athletes lined up in the central infield. It is a spectacular moment. After a pause, the runner descends to the track and runs round the stadium to the other side. Here he lights the Olympic torch. Sound recorded and mixed later recreates the gush as the flame lights. The crowds sing an Olympic hymn specially composed by Richard Strauss. The camera lingers on the Olympic emblems – the flag, the flame, the five rings. The sun sets behind the torch. The flame is lit. The Games have begun.

It is often said that the effect of this opening of the film is to highlight Hitler and to celebrate the achievement of the Third Reich. One writer has commented that 'The sequence seems to tell us that the torch of civilisation has been carried from its ancient centre, Greece, to modern Germany, watched over by a pantheon at whose apex is Hitler.'[30] In fact, this is not the effect of the English version of the film,

The runner with the flame enters the stadium

in which Hitler does not even appear until after the Greek team have marched into the stadium. Later we see him only once in close-up before he declares the Games open. Thereafter, Hitler is not seen again in the Opening Ceremony. Likewise, the Swastika flies as the torch arrives in Germany and is seen once again alongside the flags of other nations. But the most prominent flag through this opening sequence is unquestionably the Olympic flag, which dominates the stadium and the whole sequence.

There is no doubt that the grandeur of the stadium and the tens of thousands of people within it is in its way a celebration of the achievements of the Third Reich. But, as we have seen, the Nazis intended the Games to promote the 'new order' in Germany. In reality, the first twenty-two minutes of the film are relatively modest in this regard. Every Olympic film made since applauds the magnificence of the main stadium constructed for the Games. Ichikawa's film of the 1964 Tokyo Games has a hauntingly beautiful opening sequence with the rising sun and the new stadium. The 1976 film of the Montreal Games lingers lovingly around the structure of the main stadium, which was still being built at the time of the Opening Ceremony. In both the television and the film coverage of the 1984 Los Angeles Games there were far more shots of the Stars and Stripes than there were of the Swastika in 1936. So blatant did ABC Television's pro-American stance become in 1984 that the IOC had to warn the network to play a less chauvinistic role as host broadcaster of the Games. The Games are always in effect a celebration of the city and of the regime which hosts them.

Riefenstahl's film captures the powerful emotional impact of the Opening Ceremony. But purely in terms of the number of shots, the English version of the film does not elevate Hitler beyond the importance of any head of state proclaiming the Games open. Despite this, the viewer is still left with a sense of Hitler presiding over the Games. Even when he is not seen, his presence is felt.

VI
. . . .
TRACK AND FIELD

After the Prologue and the Opening Ceremony, the film moves on to the athletics competition which occupied the first week of the Games and fills Part One. The first day again begins in the awesome setting of the giant stadium, packed with spectators and dominated by the Olympic emblems. Behind the five rings, shot from a low angle and seemingly suspended in the heavens, a cloud passes through an otherwise clear sky. A montage of commentators at microphones introduce the Games in six languages. This sets up the device that will be used to provide commentary links throughout the film. There had never previously been any television coverage of the Olympic Games. In Berlin, Telefunken carried out the first television experiments with closed-circuit coverage of some of the events, relayed live to giant halls around the city. But real television coverage of the Games as a 'live' spectacle broadcast directly to people's homes did not come until after the war.[31]

Most people would have followed the Games in 1936 in the press and on the radio. Riefenstahl used radio commentators, sometimes in vision, mostly in voice-over, as a device for introducing events and naming athletes. The commentators were filmed after the Games in a studio with crowd scenes back-projected behind them to give the impression that they were reporting on the events 'live'. To the modern viewer the effect is rather bizarre. To the viewer in the late 1930s it would have been an efficient way of translating one familiar medium, radio coverage of sport, to a less familiar medium, film coverage with a commentary background. The commentator narrates the film throughout in a neutral, unemotional style which, again, would have been familiar to most radio listeners at the time.

In the German version of the film, Dr Paul Laven, the most famous radio sports announcer in Germany, was the principal commentator. The main BBC radio sports commentator of the day was Harold Abrahams, the 1924 Olympic gold medallist. As a Jew, he was probably not asked, or he refused, to provide the commentary for the English version of the film, which was read in a plummy BBC accent by Howard Marshall. His intonation is frequently over-dramatic and his commentary caused some merriment in the United States, where the same English version was shown.

The first event covered in the film is the men's discus. The event provides a direct link with ancient Greece and refers back to the moment of transition in the prologue. Now, again, the discus provides a transition from the ceremonial prologue to the sporting core of the film. After the fanfares and pageantry of the opening twenty minutes, the discus event is covered simply. Carpenter wins, giving the United States its first gold medal.

Next comes the women's discus. By following a men's event with the same event for women, the film gives an impression of sexual equality in sport that was ahead of its time. In fact, there were only six women's track and field events in the Games of 1936, against twenty-three men's events. There were no women's running events beyond 100 metres, and women were not even allowed to run the 800 metres event until 1960. Coverage of the women's discus is again low-key. Riefenstahl uses the slow-motion camera of Kurt Neubert for the first time on the throw of the Polish competitor, Wajsowna. As the soundtrack falls silent, the German Mauermayer makes her final throw, again captured in slow motion. Mauermayer wins the gold medal for Germany. The crowd cheers. Mauermayer turns and, backlit, looks into the camera smiling. In a packed stadium, the camera captures her intimate moment of victory.

The next sequence follows the women's 80 metres hurdles.[32] After two heats the finals are covered in a continuous shot. The camera is positioned in the stadium just before the finishing line. As the runners pass in front of the camera the Italian, Valla, and the German, Steuer, are neck and neck. The camera records the intensity of the struggle. Valla wins and the Italians in the crowd, most of whom seem to be wearing military uniforms, jump for joy. Riefenstahl filmed every medal ceremony but this is one of the few that actually appear in the film. As the band play the Fascist anthem 'Giovinezza', Valla receives her medal and her laurel wreath. She and Steuer, who has won the silver medal, stand on the podium, their arms held out in the Nazi salute. From the VIP box Hitler returns their salute. The film fades to black on Valla, looking like a classical deity with her laurel wreath, her arm outstretched across the frame.

In these early events Riefenstahl is already demonstrating her cinematic imagination. The heats place the event in the context of the stadium, while the finals concentrate our attention on the runners. The next event uses a device even more dramatic. During the men's hammer-throwing, the camera tracks in the opposite direction behind the athletes as they rotate to get up to speed to throw the hammer. The effect is superb. The tracking of the camera acts with the physical spinning of the athlete to project us right into the heart of the event. It was while shooting here that Guzzi Lantschner was asked by an official to move. Riefenstahl went to argue with the official, who took offence and reported her. Goebbels later accused Riefenstahl of abusing the referees.

Other shots of the hammer-throwing are taken from one of the towers that were built in the stadium. The pace of the competition builds up through the rhythm of the editing. Repeated use is made of cutaways of the crowd, especially from the tiny Kinamo cameras of Heinz von Jaworsky which were positioned around the stadium and capture the German spectators chanting in support of the German champion. In the end, to the delight of Hitler, Goebbels and Goering, Germany takes both gold and silver in the event. Both throws break the Olympic record.

The next event in the film is the 100 metres, won by the legendary black American athlete Jesse Owens. Riefenstahl says that she was pressured to play down Owens's fantastic achievement in winning four gold medals in Berlin. But there is no sense of this in the film. Rather she seems to have been attracted by the physical beauty of the young black athlete, an obsession that stayed with her throughout her life. The camera picks out his strikingly elegant figure right at the beginning of the heats. In the finals, Riefenstahl lingers on Owens as he waits, coiled in the starting position. Her cameras and editing create a study of tense concentration. It was while filming the 100 metres that Riefenstahl abandoned her 'Manuscript' that had been so carefully prepared before the Games but no longer seemed relevant. The film shows us two heats, one semi-final and the final. Owens looks unbeatable. In the semi-finals he runs magnificently and breaks the then world record with a time of 10.2 seconds, though this is disallowed for being wind-assisted. Although the other black American sprinter, Ralph Metcalfe, comes a tenth of a second behind him in second place in the final, Owens dominates the event. It was an outstanding performance by this young athlete from Alabama, who had grown up under the apartheid of the southern American states. Owens's victory marked a triumph for black Americans and began a long history of track victories that would later be used more overtly in the black American cause. But in 1936 it was enough that a black man should so dominate the track and field events. This was especially so in a country which regarded blacks as sub-human. Owens's victories were a powerful political statement in Nazi Germany and one that could not be covered up. Riefenstahl did not attempt to do so and goes against the Nazi grain by celebrating this unique achievement in the film.[33]

Hitler had behaved badly at the start of the Games. On the first day he had congratulated three German gold medal winners by publicly greeting them after their victories. The President of the IOC, Count Baillet-Latour, reminded Hitler that Olympic protocol required that he congratulate either every winner or none at all. Hitler withdrew and did not greet another athlete during the course of the Games, in public at least. It was known that the black Americans were likely to dominate the track events and doubtless Hitler could not bear the prospect of having to shake the hand of one decried by Nazi propaganda as a sub-human. None of this is seen in the film of course, but Riefenstahl indirectly refers to it. Hitler is seen in the stadium applauding German victories but does not appear in the film cheering on non-Germans, the only exception being the Italian woman Valla in the 80 metres hurdles. In its own way, this neatly captures the chauvinism of the Nazi leadership.

The next field event in the film is the women's high jump. Here Riefenstahl liberally uses slow-motion to create a rhythmic montage of running and jumping. After the first few jumps, she cuts from one camera to another, situated all round the event. This has the effect of breaking the usual grammar of film editing to lose the sense of time and place, technically known as 'crossing the line'. Riefenstahl crosses the line repeatedly, as the high jump is turned into a sort of cinematic ballet. As a pure and simple record of the event, it is confusing and sometimes jumbled. As a piece of film-making it is an enchanting interpretation of striving and achievement, triumph and failure. The Hungarian Csak wins and 16-year-old Dorothy Odam of Great Britain takes the silver. The English commentator intones, 'Bad luck, Dorothy, but well done!'

After the sophistication of different camera angles, slow-motion effects, cross-cutting and cutaways used for the women's high jump, the next event in the film is covered from one camera in a single shot. The men's 400 metres features one lap of the track. From a camera high in the stadium near the finishing line, on a long lens of perhaps 150 mm focal length, the event is captured almost in the way someone in the crowd would have seen it. On the final bend the black American Archie Williams storms through to take an unbeatable lead. In front of the camera, the British runner Godfrey Brown lunges at the tape to take the silver. In the pacing of the film, the 400 metres comes as a moment of natural drama without any of the technically achieved effects in the events surrounding it.

The men's shot is the next field event and for this the long lens of Hans Scheib captures some of the intense moments of concentration and drama. Scheib's 600 mm lens enabled him to study in close-up the stresses and strains of putting the shot. Such a lens was cumbersome and gave the operator a tiny field of action to cover. The lens could never have been used with accuracy on an event which required much movement. But the single heave of the shot putter was ideal.

The next two events show the smooth editing rhythm of *Olympia*. The 800 metres is covered from cameras on the infield area just on the bend of the track when the runners are spread out but curving inwards towards the camera. Almost certainly this was shot by Hans Ertl. His shots are intercut with the more conventionally placed cameras around the outside of the track. The Italian team cheer on their hero Lanzi, but the race is won by the giant American John Woodruff. In the triple jump, Riefenstahl uses slow-motion shots of the jumps in which the athletes seem to stay in the air for an impossibly long moment. These are intercut with long-lens shots of the jumpers about to start their run-up and shots of the crowd looking on. Japan traditionally dominated this event and caused no surprises by taking gold and silver medals.

The long jump, which follows, was one of the highlights of the Games and Riefenstahl makes of it one of the most exciting pieces of sport ever shot and edited for the cinema. The competition finally came down to a titanic struggle between Lutz Long, the German, and Jesse Owens. It became a competition not just between two men but between two ideologies. Long, the clean-cut Aryan, was jumping for Hitler and Nazism. Owens, the black man from an underprivileged background, was jumping – symbolically – on behalf of the whole black race to refute the absurdity of Nazi racial values. Spectators who were there at the time were able to recall later the intense emotions aroused by the event, and the film fully lives up to the moment itself.[34]

Lutz Long jumps 7.54 metres and takes the lead. Then Owens jumps 7.74 metres, a new Olympic record. Long edges ahead with a jump of 7.84 metres. Owens responds with 7.87 metres. Long comes up for his final jump. He pauses at the beginning of his run-up. Every eye in the crowd is watching him. It almost seems as though the fate of the Reich hangs on his jump. In slow motion from a low-angle camera, perhaps Guzzi Lantschner's in a pit next to the jump, we see him run up and take off. He flies through the air, his legs spinning. He jumps 7.87 metres. It's a new European record and equals Owens's jump. The film

Lutz Long in the long jump

cuts back to real time as the crowd erupt. Grown men hug each other. The Führer rocks back and forth in delight.

Then Owens comes up for his final jump. The American spectators are in agony. A woman wrings the programme she is holding. There is a side profile of Owens as he steels himself for the greatest moment in his career. The shot is held for what seems like forever. Everything goes silent. In an immensely dramatic use of sound, only the wind rattles the cords of the flags high above on the stadium roof. Owens starts his run-up. The film cuts to Long watching the jump, his head turning as he watches Owens run. It then cuts back to a slow-motion shot of Owens jumping from the same low angle. He bounds through the air, and as he lands his forward momentum is so great that he seems to spring onwards. His jump records an astonishing 8.06 metres. Owens wins. Democracy triumphs over fascism. The Americans in the crowd are ecstatic. The Stars and Stripes are waved with a new frenzy. There is not a shot of anyone who appears to be German. For all we know, Hitler has walked out in disgust. Owens has

Jesse Owens in the long jump

won with a jump that is nearly 20 cms longer than his last jump and sets a new world record. It wasn't until 1960 that any Olympic athlete jumped as far again.

Every ounce of drama is squeezed out of the competition between these two men. The film dramatically, even lovingly, records the outstanding athleticism of Jesse Owens. And it chronicles the great sportsmanship of Lutz Long. If Riefenstahl was ever told that she should not feature the triumphs of Owens, she blatantly disregarded the instruction. While Goebbels's rabble-rousing newspaper *Der Angriff* refused even to list the medal-scoring achievements of the black athletes, Riefenstahl's *Olympia* puts the record straight. There can be no doubt who was the greatest athlete of the Games, and in *Olympia* Riefenstahl celebrates his achievements.

After the high drama of the long jump, the 1500 metres comes as a stark contrast. There is a close shot of the runners at the starting line and then the entire race, all three and three-quarter laps of the track, is covered in one shot from a camera high in the stadium. There is not a single edit in the sequence; and the race does not need it. It was a magnificent battle between Luigi Beccali of Italy, Glen Cunningham of the United States, Eric Ny of Sweden and Jack Lovelock of New Zealand. In a superb finish, Lovelock ran away with the gold and broke the world record. The sequence ends with close-ups of a delighted Lovelock. 'God Save the King' is played and the crowd stands, hands held out in salute. This epic race is perfectly placed in the film and treated with a brave simplicity.

The men's high jump begins with a sequence of limbering up, of muscles being massaged and of nervous anticipation. Jumps are shown in slow motion as the field gradually narrows and the bar goes higher and higher. The film captures the concentration of the jumpers as they motivate themselves to jump ever higher. Again there is a powerful use of sound as the stadium appears to fall silent for the final few jumps. Neubert's slow-motion pit cameras are used to great effect. Cornelius Johnson takes another gold for black America, his team-mate Dave Albritton takes the silver. Another blow for the Nazi theories on race.

The treatment of the men's javelin changes the mood considerably. There is virtually no stadium sound and the event is cut to Windt's music, less like a fanfare than before. Scheib's telephoto lens captures some intense moments. Neubert's slow-motion camera records the effort of throwing. Riefenstahl cuts back to a wide shot of the javelin flying through the air and landing in real time. The mixture of angles, lenses and speeds cut with the music creates a beautiful symphony to the javelin. Gerhard Stock wins for Germany, defeating the Finns who had dominated the event, to the delight of Hitler, Goebbels and Goering. The crowd sing 'Deutschland über Alles' with gusto.

The 10,000 metres begins with a close-up of the starter's pistol being fired. The treatment is straightforward, mostly from the camera position in the stand. There are some of the best crowd shots in the film here. American servicemen, Japanese visitors, a group of Indian women, German officers, and spectators of every race and colour watch a gruelling twenty-five laps of the track. Three lanky Finns, Salminen, Askola and Iso-Hollo, and a diminutive Japanese runner, Kohei Murakosa, battle it out. The Finns take the first three places, confirming that nation's mastery of the long-distance track events in the inter-war years.

The pole vault begins with a montage of running up and vaulting, cut with music. One camera is high above the bar looking down on it; another is way behind the pit looking back on the vaulters, and a third is alongside the jump itself. Slow motion and real-time shots are again cut together. The event began in the morning but continued into the evening, becoming a dramatic struggle between five vaulters, three Americans and two Japanese. As the sun went down, Riefenstahl's cameramen had to stop filming. She was not allowed to use the bright arc-lights that would have been needed to obtain an exposure – the officials said they would disturb the vaulters – and missed the finish to this dramatic event. Undaunted, she approached the American and Japanese vaulters the next day and asked them if they would return to the stadium and recreate their final jumps for the cameras. They all agreed. All the officials returned too, and the tense final vaults were restaged for the film. Interestingly, the result was the same as it had been in the real final. Earle Meadows won for the United States. The sequence that Riefenstahl shot at night is interesting but lacks the intensity of genuine competition. Oe of Japan looks far too relaxed, the American vaulters are clearly having a lot of fun in the reconstruction, and the crowd scenes are absurdly overstaged. The reconstructed event feels as artificial as it was, and this is one of the least successful sequences in the film. The final shot of Meadows, supposedly on the victory podium, goes through a long dissolve to the Stars and Stripes, filling the frame as it ripples in the wind. This device was later developed to great effect by ABC Television during their coverage of the 1984 Los Angeles Games.

On the final day of the athletics competition the weather was good and the shadows were long inside the stadium. The three relay events were followed by the marathon. Germany was favourite to win the women's 4×100 metres relay but the baton was dropped at the fourth changeover and the American team went on to win. Hitler and Goebbels, who had been yelling with excitement during the race, don't hide their disappointment. In the men's 4×100 metres, Owens, helps to give the USA a big lead and wins his fourth gold medal of the Games. The American team broke the world record with a time that stood for twenty years.

Dissolve of the Stars and Stripes over Earle Meadows

The men's 4×400 metres relay is one of the legendary races of British athletics history. The first lap by Freddie Wolff leaves Britain third. In the second leg Godfrey Rampling runs a superb race and on the final bend he charges past the American and Canadian runners to give Britain the lead. In a continuous shot, without edits, the camera follows Bill Roberts in third leg as he fights off a fierce challenge from O'Brian of the USA. A trackside shot picks up Godfrey Brown anxiously waiting for the baton. Again without editing, the film follows Brown in the last leg as he sprints down the final straight to pull away from the American who was catching him. Britain takes gold. The film treatment captures every moment of excitement in this most dramatic of finals.

The marathon presented Riefenstahl with great problems. She had devoted much time before the Games to preparing for this event in which fifty-eight runners would run over twenty-six miles through the city and suburbs of Berlin in two and a half hours. The race begins with vast wide shots of the stadium and the track outside, with the long line of runners spreading out. Windt's music sets up a heavy beat that drives

The marathon

through much of the race. Outside Berlin there are tracking shots of the runners. As the race continues, the heat takes its toll. Some competitors are reduced to walking. Others, like Zabala of Argentina, drop out altogether. The music intensifies, and the shots become point-of-view images of the runners. Wheat in the wind at the side of the route. Shadows of men running. Big close-ups of faces. Trees overhead. Arms in motion. Walter Frentz's dramatic shots, taken during training sessions, look down at the runners' feet. The music pounds out in time with the running feet. The viewer almost feels the exhaustion. There is a long dissolve to the stadium. Trumpeters sound a fanfare. The mood changes instantly. Kitei Son, a Korean, runs in to take gold for Japan (Korea being then part of the Japanese empire).[35] Ernie Harper takes the silver for Britain and Nan the bronze for Japan. The film records the first ten runners as they cross the line and collapse. Some of the shots dissolve out of focus. Riefenstahl's fourteen-minute record of the marathon is a film within a film. The inclusion of the footage shot before the race itself builds an artistic impression of the marathon which makes the sequence more than just a chronicle of the event. It creates a statement about achievement and endurance and takes the viewer right inside the race itself. Rarely has a marathon been treated with such imagination on film.

Part One ends with a short montage of Olympic emblems. As Windt's music reaches its crescendo, the giant Olympic bell tolls. From the stadium the film dissolves to the symbol of Olympism, the five-ring flag, and then slowly fades to black.

VII

. . . .

FESTIVAL OF BEAUTY

Riefenstahl called the first part of her film *Fest der Völker* (*Festival of the People*) and the second part *Fest der Schönheit* (*Festival of Beauty*). The two parts were originally intended to be screened as separate films, and *Festival of Beauty* was premiered six weeks after Part One. But the film is usually seen today as a single epic in two distinct parts.

Part Two has its own prologue, shot in and around the Olympic Village. It begins with misty, moody shots of water, leaves, light reflecting on the surface of a lake. Dawn. A spider's web is lit by the rising sun. Drops of water are silhouetted on a leaf. A beetle crawls through the undergrowth. A heron flaps its wing. Violins slowly awake on the soundtrack. A camera picks up the athletes' dwellings. The sunlight filters through the trees. As the music takes up a more steady rhythm, we see the outline of joggers running beside a lake. Through the morning mist the shape of men running in a line forms more clearly. A wide shot shows the athletes running along the lakeside. This image of running echoes the prologue of Part One where runners carry the Olympic flame across the Greek countryside. The runners cross a bridge and disappear into the woodlands. Naked, they run from the lake into a sauna. The steam of the sauna replaces the dawn mist. Riefenstahl's preoccupation with the beauty of the human body, particularly the male physique, comes through again. The men massage each other, and beat each other with birch twigs. There are close, sensuous shots of limbs, muscles, faces. The naked men dive into the lake. Others sit on the wooden balcony. Man and nature in harmony. The sun is up now. The day has begun.

Opening of Part II: men in the sauna ... (above)
... and in the lake (overleaf)

Suddenly the Village is full. Athletes from all the nations mingle and exercise. They warm up, they run, they box, they jump. Men play hockey, some play football, others basketball. As we see many of the sports, so we see many of the nations – Italians, Peruvians, Indians, Colombians. Black men and white men, Asians and Westerners. The music shifts from a gentle symphony to a jazz piano. People are having fun. Discus throwers and shot putters practise their skills – again an echo from the prologue of Part One. Hurdlers hurdle and javelin throwers throw. A man reads in the sun. Flags fly protectively overhead. The athletes of the world are ready.[36]

The women's gymnastic teams march into the giant Dietrich-Eckart open-air theatre behind their national flags. The men's teams follow. The martial beat of the music for once creates a comic effect. After some warm-up exercises on the single bar, we see impressive displays on the parallel bars. Some of this was shot during pre-Games training. The sequence with the American gymnast Consetta Carrucio was probably shot after the Games, since the camera is too close to be allowed during competition and the cameraman was not to know that she would win in her section. A long sequence with the German gymnast Karl Schwarzmann on the high bar was also probably shot after the Games. The gymnastics sequence is long and slow. It relies upon the extensive use of slow motion and the careful synchronisation of the editing with the music. Shots are held for a long time. The men and women are graceful and balletic, displaying remarkable qualities of power and control. This lyrical sequence was shot by Guzzi Lantschner and Neubert's principal assistant Eberhard von der Heyden on the slow-motion camera. The sequence ends with a brief display of women's group gymnastics. This event has fallen out of fashion because it is indelibly associated with the health and beauty, open-air philosophy of National Socialism. There are a few shots of women moving in unison, a reference to the 'eurhythmics' of the opening prologue. The camera mixes to wider and wider shots until there is an extraordinary pan across the field outside the main stadium, in which 10,000 women in long straight lines are seen waving and moving together.

The next sequence begins with the commentator, who announces that we are in Kiel where the yachting events will take place. The competition was supervised by the German navy. From tracking shots we pass the sailing boats in their moorings and then there is a cut to a shot of a German battlecruiser. Hitler is on board watching the races. All filming at Kiel was done by Walter Frentz, the water-sports specialist. Very little of the sequence in the final film shows much of the genuine races, except for one or two long shots and some lovely aerial shots of the six-metre yachts out in Kiel harbour. These were taken from a balloon moored to a German minesweeper and involved some danger as the balloon, filled with hydrogen, had to be kept well away from the hot exhaust from the minesweeper's chimney. However, most of the footage used was shot by Frentz in June and July when he filmed aboard several of the yachts during practice races. These images capture the thrill of sailing, as the crews push themselves to the limit to extract every extra second of speed. Without these shots the sequence would convey nothing of the skill and challenge of the sport. Because of the visual limitations in covering yachting races, there is usually very little of these events in most Olympic films.

The Modern Pentathlon was an event for the military which had been dominated by the Swedish army since its appearance in the Games in 1912. It consisted of five different events and was spread out over the first week of the Games in a variety of locations around Berlin. Only three events are included in the film.[37] The first was horse-riding, and a number of cameramen were positioned on the three-mile cross-country course at Doberitz. In the pistol shooting section it is clear that some of the competitors were asked to hold up their pistols after the event and pretend to shoot just for the camera; these shots are unconvincing. The final event in the film is the cross-country run. The German army, represented by Georg Handrick, took the gold medal, wresting the event from the Swedes who for the first time did not take any of the medals. Then follow sequences from the finals of three team games. In the hockey final India defeated Germany 8–1. The polo final between Argentina and Mexico was played on the field behind the main stadium. Hitler was in the ground to watch Italy play Austria in the soccer final, in which the Italians scored the winning goal in extra time. Coverage of all three events is unremarkable if thorough, with at least three cameras at each game.

Treatment of the three-day individual equestrian event which

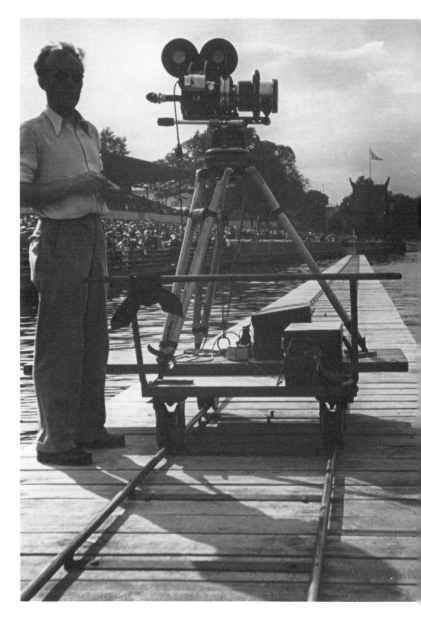

76   The pier on which a cameraman followed the finish to the rowing events at Grünau

follows is quite different. The filming is tight and dramatic, and the event itself caused considerable controversy. Guzzi Lantschner used longer lenses than had been used to film the Modern Pentathlon and the riding has a sense of pace and drama that was missing before. Windt's music neatly underlies the whole sequence, the violins providing the pace with the trumpets occasionally erupting after a successful jump. There are outstanding displays of horsemanship here, but the filming records some disastrous falls, especially at the water-jump where there were a few bad injuries. Again, slow motion is used to capture the drama of some of these jumps, with horses jumping a fence into water that can be seen to be of uneven depth. There was much criticism that the course was too tough, and three horses had to be destroyed. Of fifty starters only twenty-seven finished the course. The Germans won both the team and the individual event, in which the winning horse, 'Nurmi', was ridden by Ludwig Stubbendorf.

The 100 kilometres cycling road race begins with panning wide shots as the riders head off on their long route around Potsdam to the east of the city. But the final few kilometres are covered by tracking shots taken from a motorised vehicle on a parallel carriageway. These shots convey the intensity of the competition as the teams try to pass each other. Again, footage taken before or after the events gets right into the race and there are low-angle shots looking up at riders, close-ups of wheels spinning and point-of-view shots of passing trees. Robert Charpentier wins the individual event for France, and the French win the team gold also in a close finish that ended with a pile-up on the finishing line.

The rowing events from Grünau feature next. The shots here were wider than Riefenstahl had wanted and lack the intensity that she achieved with coverage of other sports. The coxless fours race shows the difficulties the camera team encountered: at the finish, when the German team came through to win, the British team in second place cannot even be seen. Coverage of the finals of the Eights is transformed by the incorporation of material shot by Heinz von Jaworsky before the Games from inside the boats. There are also some exciting long-lens shots of the German and Swiss teams taken from the bank. The effect is underscored by the brilliant use of sound (all recorded eighteen months later in the studio, of course) as we hear the coxes shouting on the teams in their different languages. This investment in extra film does justice to one of the closest Olympic rowing finals ever, with five of the six teams within a length of each other at the finish. The American team won by a yard over the Italians, with the Germans third. As the 'Stars and Stripes' is played there is a lovely shot of the victory wreath being passed through the boat by the exhausted but happy American rowers.

Windt's Olympic fanfare then heralds some dramatic aerial shots of the main stadium. As the crowd take their seats, the commentator announces that we are now to see the Decathlon, one of the major events of the Games in which the United States was very strong and the Germans had high hopes. The Decathlon consists of ten events on the track and field spread over two days. Although it is one of the supreme events of the athletics programme, Riefenstahl decided not to use it in Part One of the film because there would be too much repetition of the track and field events already covered there. So she placed the Decathlon in the middle of Part Two. This works well, taking the film back to the awe-inspiring setting of the main stadium for one of the blue-ribbon events of the Olympic Games.

Before the events start, the film picks out Glen Morris of the United States as one of the hopefuls. Riefenstahl admits in her memoirs that she fell in love with Morris during the shooting of *Olympia* and had a brief affair with him. She describes how he had embraced her after the medal ceremony in the middle of the stadium 'in front of a hundred thousand spectators'. After the Games she asked him back to Berlin to reshoot some scenes. They spent a few days together and Riefenstahl says she had never experienced such passion. Eventually Morris had to return with the American team to the United States. The Decathlon is also significant in that during the filming Riefenstahl spotted Erwin Huber, the German champion, whom she approached after the Games to play the part of the discus thrower in the Prologue because she thought he looked so much like Myron's statue. Huber agreed and plays a memorable role in the film.

The Decathlon is treated in a way quite unlike the other events in Part Two, with the radio announcer introducing and commenting on each event, mostly on camera in front of the back-projected shots of the stadium. The first event is the 100 metres, followed by the long jump.

The coverage includes a dramatic close shot from a pit very near the sand where the jumpers land. Next comes the shot put, entirely covered in slow motion. At the high jump, Morris comes into the front ranking of the event. After the 400 metres at the end of the first day, Robert Clark of America has a lead of two points over Morris, with Jack Parker third and Erwin Huber in tenth position.

The second day begins with the 110 metres hurdles. There are some brief shots of the discus and some lovely slow-motion footage of the pole vault and the javelin. The 1500 metres, the climax of the competition, happened too late in the day to be filmed and was restaged for Riefenstahl by Morris, Huber and a few other competitors. A rather unreal high-angle panning shot follows Morris and Huber as they recreated the last lap of the race. Morris won decisively, taking the Decathlon with a new world record and proving himself as the finest all-round athlete of the Games. The Decathlon is always difficult to capture on film and Riefenstahl succeeds by using staged material, particularly the close shots of Morris, intercut with actuality footage.

Glen Morris in the Decathlon

The final sequence of sporting events takes place in the swimming arena situated alongside the main stadium. A new musical refrain sets the scene with a low-angle tracking shot behind the crowds gathered in the open-air poolside seating. This beautiful scene-setting shot was taken from a large crane constructed and operated by Hasso Hartnagel. All the swimming and diving events took place in the second week of the Games when the sun shone continuously. In the film we first see the women's springboard diving competition, in which real-time shots of the diving give way to slow-motion shots, first from the poolside and then from a camera position above the diving board. Some of these shots clearly derive from the footage shot by Hans Ertl before the Games began, while the shots of Dorothy Poynton-Hill were just as clearly taken after the competition because the stadium behind her is empty. After several dives, the film cuts to the underwater camera Ertl had constructed specially for the competition. The underwater shots edited with Windt's (for once) lyrical music create a very pleasing effect. The winner of the event is 16-year-old Margery Gestring of the

Cameraman Hasso Hartnagel on a travelling crane films the shot which opens the swimming sequence

United States, and Americans also take silver and bronze. Instead of another medal ceremony, we see the delighted teenager signing autographs by the pool.

The next event is the men's 200 metres breast-stroke final. The first two lengths are filmed from a poolside camera on tracks built and operated by Fritz von Friedl. Hitler cheers on the German swimmer Ernst Sietas. The film then cuts to some of the big close-ups by Hans Ertl which were taken before or after the event: some of his most successful shots, taken with a camera held underwater from a rubber dinghy just ahead of the swimmers. Apparently when Ertl was shooting this material he was so close that the Japanese swimmer Detsuo Hamuro kept brushing his camera lens with his hand. The race ends with a photo-finish between Hamuro and Sietas. The camera is on Hamuro, still in the water, when he is told that he has won.[38]

The film's treatment of the men's 100 metres freestyle is by comparison very plain. The whole race is seen in two shots. The tracking poolside camera covers the first length and a high-angle wide

Cameraman Hans Ertl takes close-ups from the rubber dingy during swimming practice

shot covers the final fifty metres. The women's 100 metres freestyle is covered in a single high-angle shot from the top of the stadium. Again, Riefenstahl shows her control of pacing and rhythm, in what she called the 'architecture' of the film, by cutting these two events so simply in the midst of more visually complex sequences. It seems that she had an abundance of material from the swimming events and not much of it was used in the final film. Ertl became more and more bold with his underwater shots and even captured, in training, the great American swimmer and world-record holder Adolf Kiefer, doing a turn. Ertl was in the next lane as Kiefer swam towards him above the water level, and dropped below the water level as the swimmer performed his turn. Ertl was delighted with the shot, but Kiefer does not even appear in the film.[39] Perhaps by the time Riefenstahl was editing the swimming events she was running out of time or energy.

The men's highboard diving which follows is one of the most beautiful sequences in the film. Here the genius of Ertl's camerawork captures the grace and athleticism of the divers. Windt's music and

Riefenstahl's montage help the sequence to transcend mere reportage. The sequence becomes a five-minute hymn to the beauty of the human body in motion. There is not a word of commentary throughout. Only the first few shots are in real time, then we see divers in slow motion from the trackside, from above the board and from below the water. The sequence includes a shot that Ertl struggled to get, starting above the water looking up at the diver and then plunging below the water level with him. At least half the material for this sequence was shot after the competition – some of the dives are clearly made in an empty stadium. After a while the angles become more extreme, the editing more abstract. Divers dive, but do not fall. There are at least two shots played in reverse. Bodies fall through the air; other bodies spin and rotate, timelessly, as though defying gravity. The last few divers never reach the water, left in the air performing their gyrations. The sequence is without question one of the most imaginative celebrations of the elegance of the human form ever put together on film.

Olympia ends with a short closing montage of flags and of the stadium at night. Because the actual Closing Ceremony took place during the evening there was not enough light for Riefenstahl to obtain good material, and she used models in a studio. These shots, which show the dipping of the flags of the nations and the fading of the Olympic flame, are unconvincing, and Windt's music is at its most pompous. The final image is a simulation of the searchlights which Albert Speer used during the Closing Ceremony to create a colonnade of light reaching into the sky. The camera slowly tilts up into the sky where the searchlight beams merge in a dome of light. The film fades to black on the halo-like effect above the main stadium. As Riefenstahl wrote in her memoirs: 'Who could have imagined on that night that only a few years later these searchlights would be looking for enemy aircraft in the skies over Berlin, and at the searchlights and in the aircraft the young people who would do battle were those who had fought in such friendship here?'

VIII

AFTERMATH

The premiere of the German version of the film, *Olympische Spiele*, was held on 20 April 1938, at the Ufa-Palast am Zoo in Berlin. The day was Hitler's forty-ninth birthday and at the gala event there were gathered almost all the leading figures of the Nazi state. Outside the theatre the red swastika banners alternated with the five rings of the white Olympic flag. An ss guard of Hitler's elite bodyguard were stationed around the cinema. The Party, the government, the military, the film industry, the International Olympic Committee and the entire diplomatic corps in Berlin were represented at the highest level. The screening was an outstanding success. Hitler presented Riefenstahl with a bouquet of while lilacs and red roses. The Greek envoy presented her with an olive twig from Olympia by order of the Crown Prince of Greece. Rarely has there been a film premiere like it.

Riefenstahl spent the next six months attending gala premieres throughout the capitals of Europe. She met royalty, heads of state, prime ministers and sports leaders. Everywhere she went she travelled as an honorary ambassador of the Reich, and she later received a fee from the Propaganda Ministry for the months she spent promoting the film and, through it, the Reich itself. In every city she became a celebrity. She showed the film in Vienna (Austria had just been annexed to Germany), Zurich, Athens, Brussels (where King Leopold publicly flirted with her), Belgrade, Paris, Copenhagen, Stockholm and Helsinki. At the Venice Film Festival in September, the film was awarded the festival's first prize, the 'Coppa Mussolini'. The British and American representatives went home peeved. They had wanted Disney's *Snow White and the Seven Dwarfs* to win and felt the award had been political. The grand tour continued to Rome, Oslo and back to Sweden. Everywhere the film caused a stir and most reviews were enthusiastic.

Slowly, of course, political events were to take over. As Hitler became more menacing, so support for the kind of Germany portrayed in the Olympic film waned. In September 1938, with the agreement of Chamberlain and Daladier, Hitler occupied part of Czechoslovakia. On 'Kristallnacht' in November, Jewish stores were looted, synagogues were burnt and Jews were beaten up all over Germany. Although an English version of the film was produced, called *Olympia*, it was not commercially distributed in Britain until after the war. Riefenstahl made a fruitless trip to the United States and was boycotted in Hollywood by all the major studios. Walt Disney was the only studio executive willing to see her and even he was not willing to screen the film. In June 1939, the International Olympic Committee awarded Riefenstahl the Olympic Gold Medal.[40] This was to be the last award the film received. The dark clouds of war now cast a shadow over the future of the film.

During the war several of the cameramen who had worked on *Olympia* contributed to the German film propaganda effort. Walter Frentz was attached to Hitler's headquarters for part of the war. Eberhard von der Heyden, who had shot some of the beautiful slow-motion sequences of the gymnasts in action, was killed during the Crete campaign. Riefenstahl herself did not produce any propaganda films during the war. She spent some years trying to shoot and edit a feature film based on the opera *Tiefland*. She achieved notoriety at one point when she cast some gypsies as extras, apparently saving them, but only temporarily, from concentration camps.

The history of *Olympia* in the years after the war is equally complex. Riefenstahl was arrested and detained first by the French and then by us Intelligence Officers on charges relating to her pro-Nazi activities. Although released by 1948, she spent several years trying to clear her name and return to film-making and also to regain the negatives of *Olympia* which had been taken from her. None of the film-makers of the Third Reich were put on trial, but Riefenstahl was investigated not only for having made *Triumph of the Will* and *Olympia* but also because of the allegations about the closeness of her relationship with Hitler. She repeatedly proclaimed her political innocence and started to prepare her version of events which, as noted, often differs markedly from that of the surviving records. As part of her de-Nazification process she re-edited a shorter version of *Olympia*. In the Federal Republic of Germany in the late 1950s there was an almost hysterical fear that if the public saw Nazi flags and the image of Hitler again there would be a resurgence of support for National Socialism. The re-edited version of the film was intended to prevent any such revival.

By the early 1960s, Riefenstahl had the master negatives back in her possession and obtained rights in the film from Transit-Film, which had been established by the German government to control the exploitation of all film material produced during the Nazi period. The situation with regard to what is legally known as 'enemy property' is complex and differs from country to country. Riefenstahl has taken advantage of this confusion and claims that she owns the copyright in *Olympia* in all its versions worldwide.[41] She has not been slow to use the courts to forward this claim and on several occasions she has threatened film-makers, distributors and broadcasters like the BBC with legal action.

Even if *Olympia* has now won some respectability, Riefenstahl herself has not. Protests have prevented her appearance at many events. She has been stopped from attending screenings at the National Film Theatre in London and at an Olympic Week in Lausanne, Switzerland. In 1956 Riefenstahl began shooting a colour documentary film about the black slave trade in Africa but was seriously injured in a road accident and spent a year in hospital. The project was called off. In the 1960s and 70s she returned to Africa to photograph tribes like the Masai Mara. Her photographs reveal all the sensual appreciation of the physique of the human body she had celebrated in *Olympia*. During the 1972 Munich Olympic Games, Riefenstahl returned to the Olympic arena as a photographer for *The Times*. At the time of writing she is approaching her ninetieth birthday, living in Munich and still keen to defend her reputation, issue writs and collect money from anybody anywhere who might want to make use of a few frames of *Olympia*.

In the years since the Berlin Olympics there have been many attempts to produce films of the Games. Nowadays, the IOC authorises the making of an 'official' film at each Games, and the question of who owns what rights is clearly laid down from the start.[42] In 1948 the Games were held in London. The British film industry responded by organising its 'greatest combined operation' ever. A new company was formed by the Rank Organisation, the Olympic Games Film Company Ltd, and Castleton Knight was appointed producer with a budget of a quarter of a million pounds. A large team of cameramen, editors, sound engineers and laboratory staff was assembled from all branches of the industry.[43] Clearly the model for the organisation of the film came from

Berlin and most of the team viewed and examined *Olympia*. The result is an interesting British Technicolor documentary, but the film has absolutely none of the flair or visual quality of Riefenstahl's epic.

The only recent Olympic film to come anywhere near *Olympia* in terms of cinematic quality was Kon Ichikawa's film of the 1964 Tokyo Olympic Games, *Tokyo Olympiad*. The film was made in the wide-screen format and Ichikawa had all the advantages of nearly thirty years of technological advance. Extremely long lenses were used that would have astonished Hans Scheib. Slow-motion techniques were pushed to speeds that Kurt Neubert and his team could only dream about. Indeed the film's release ushered in a spirited debate within the athletics establishment as to whether runners actually breathe or not during the 100 metres sprint, so extraordinary were the images Ichikawa presented of the runners in action. *Tokyo Olympiad* is a dazzling film. It evokes the spirit of a Japan returning to world favour after the disgrace of the war and captures the magnificence of the spectacle. The opening sequence of the rising sun over Tokyo has to rival Riefenstahl's Prologue. But the film also captures many intimate, personal moments as the world's greatest athletes compete.

Since 1964 and the advent of worldwide communication satellites, the Olympics have become a global television spectacle. There have been many interesting films, like *Visions of Eight* in which eight top directors each took a theme and made a mini-documentary about the Munich Games in 1972. In 1976 the National Film Board of Canada made an observational documentary using handheld material shot during the Montreal Games. Bud Greenspan has produced more than one fascinating film account of recent Games. *Sixteen Days of Glory*, the film of the Los Angeles 1984 Games, is his best contribution to the 'genre'. But all these films have in one sense or another been defined by their relationship to the television coverage of the Games. Now viewers can see dramatic close-ups, slow-motion action, instant replays and more camera angles than anyone would have thought possible in 1936, and they can see it *live* in every country in the world. So the official film of the Games has to offer a new perspective and a different sort of record of the Olympics. At his best, as in 1984, Bud Greenspan has provided a view of the Games that ABC Television viewers never saw. But as most of these films now are not made for cinema release but for video distribution, they have become more like extended television reviews than major examples of screen art.

By any comparison *Olympia* remains one of the best, if not the best, sports film ever made. The fact that Riefenstahl so liberally used material that had been shot before or after the Games outside the competitions themselves makes no difference to the film as a work of art. If it diminishes the film as a record of the Games, it strengthens it as a film that goes beyond reportage of the event to work on a higher level altogether. Riefenstahl loved the human body and especially the male body. The framing she asked of her cameramen, the montage she struggled with for over a year, the rhythm and the momentum of her film all amount to a celebration of physical beauty and athletic prowess. The Olympic Games are about striving and struggle, endurance and achievement. *Olympia* catches this spirit in countless moments of effort and triumph. Riefenstahl makes of these moments a magnificent vision of the Games and her work adds up to a unique achievement in the history of the cinema.

But there are still the accusations of political propaganda to answer. Although Riefenstahl created a superb vision of the Games, none of this would have been possible had not the Berlin Games been the spectacle they were. And there is no doubt that the Games were designed by the Nazi leadership to achieve political ends. Because at this point in the mid-1930s, Hitler and his cohorts wanted to promote Nazi Germany as a friendly, peace-loving nation, they decided to put enormous resources into the organisation of the Games. The Berlin Olympics were on a scale that marked them out from all previous Games. The stadia were awe-inspiring. The facilities for spectators were unparalleled. The Olympic Village offered the male athletes of the world unprecedented comforts and privileges. And the Nazis did not want this just to be seen and appreciated by a few tens of thousands of visitors to Berlin. They wanted it to be admired by millions worldwide. Hence large sums of money were invested in the film, and when it was finished the government made every effort to promote it and its chief architect throughout Europe. The Nazis wanted *Olympia* to be made and they wanted it to be seen.

This is the true propaganda motive behind *Olympia*. As I have said, Riefenstahl acquired a form of independence from the Propaganda

Ministry, but only through her closer alliance with the Führer. All her authority finally came directly from Hitler. He wanted her to make the film, he went along with her plans for its shooting; he supported her in her disputes with his own Propaganda Minister when the Games were over. By this strange paradox, Riefenstahl was able to keep the demands of Dr Goebbels at arm's length, and she has never ceased telling everyone this ever since. So the great athletic triumphs of Jessie Owens, Archie Williams and Cornelius Johnson are well represented. Although there are many Germany victories in the film, the Germans were in fact very successful in the Games. They won more medals than any other nation in Berlin. Judged purely in terms of its sports coverage, *Olympia* is without doubt a fair record of the Games.

Riefenstahl has always said that the film is not intentionally propagandist, that she was not trying through the film to promote the values of National Socialism. I, for one, believe her on this score. Had she been a committed Nazi she would have behaved differently and made another film. But that is not to say that the film is therefore *un*political. *Olympia* is an intensely political film. It was set up for political motives, it describes an immensely political event. It was made and promoted with government money using several agencies of the Nazi state. Let's not pretend otherwise, as Riefenstahl has done for fifty years. Instead, let's applaud the film for what it does. It transcends the political setting from which it was born. It glorifies physical beauty and sporting prowess. It is remarkably imaginative in its concept and its realisation. Riefenstahl led and inspired a creative team to achieve standards for Olympic film-making which have set the agenda for sports films ever since. Rarely, if ever, with all the advances in film technology since 1936, have these standards been surpassed. We should by now be able not only to accept *Olympia* as a political film and to enjoy it as one of the greatest sports documentaries ever made, but also to see it as a film that goes beyond both of these labels. *Olympia* remains as one of the cinema's most remarkable and powerful achievements.

NOTES

....

1 Peter Diamond, NBC Olympics co-Ordinator, in *Selling the Games*, a documentary produced by Flashback Television for Channel Four in 1987. The soccer World Cup is viewed by millions in many nations, but in some parts of the world it has far less appeal. An American space launch is watched by millions in the Western world but not much in Asia or Africa. But the Olympic Games is one of the few genuinely global television spectacles.
2 See Taylor Downing, 'The First Olympic Games on Film', in *Olympic Review* no. 227 (Lausanne: The International Olympic Committee, September 1986).
3 This material is now held by Sveriges Television in Stockholm, who have edited it into several full-length features about the Games in recent decades.
4 Quoted in Andrew Sarris (ed.), *Interviews with Film Directors* (Indianapolis: Bobbs Merrill, 1968).
5 Ernst Jäger, who was the Press Chief on the making of *Olympia*, later defected to the United States and wrote a series of articles for the *Hollywood Tribune* entitled 'How Leni Riefenstahl became Hitler's girlfriend'. Later he made up with Riefenstahl and retracted these pieces. During the 1950s he wrote supportively about her to the German government. Budd Schulberg wrote a series of articles in the American press in 1946 about Riefenstahl and Hitler, calling her a 'Nazi Pin-Up Girl'. Riefenstahl denied all these accusations during her interrogations by US Seventh Army Intelligence officers after the war and has always denied them publicly. However, such claims, no matter what inspired them, have a tendency to stick.
6 Ernst 'Putzi' Hanfstängl, *Hitler – The Missing Years* (Philadelphia: J.B. Lippincott, 1957).

7 In Leif Furhammar and Folke Isaksons, *Politics and Film* (London: Studio Vista, 1971), the authors estimate that out of 1,097 feature films made in Germany between 1933 and 1945 only 96 were actually instigated by the Ministry of Propaganda. After the war, the Allied Control Commission listed 141 feature films made during this period as politically dubious.
8 Interview with Robert Gardner in *Film Comment*, Winter 1965.
9 There is a full description of *Victory of Faith* and of the making of the film by Martin Loiperdinger and David Culbert in 'Leni Riefenstahl, the SA, and the Nazi Party Rally Films, Nuremberg 1933–34: "Sieg des Glaubens" and "Triumph des Willens" ', in *The Historical Journal of Film, Radio and Television*, vol. 8 no. 1, 1988. From this account it can be seen that *Victory of Faith* was a much more lavish production than Riefenstahl later remembered, and included several sequences which closely anticipated *Triumph of the Will*.
10 Riefenstahl later described some aspects of the making of this film in *Hinter den Kulissen des Reichsparteitagfilms* (Munich: 1935).
11 By Furhammar and Isaksson in *Politics and Film*.
12 For instance in *Politics and Film*, pp. 104–11; in Erik Barnouw, *Documentary – A History of the Non-Fiction Film* (Oxford: Oxford University Press, 1974), pp. 101–5; in David Stewart Hull, *Film in the Third Reich* (New York: Simon and Schuster, 1973), pp. 73–6.
13 *Triumph of the Will*, like *Olympia*, has been cut and re-used over and over again, providing stock shots for countless compilational film-makers to produce their own interpretations of the Nazi era. *Triumph of the Will* has had one history as the film made by Riefenstahl, and another history as a source of material for quite different films about fascism and the Third Reich.

14 She said this in interviews with the *New York Times* as late as 1972.

15 This account is largely based on Riefenstahl's memoirs, as yet unpublished in English, *Memoiren* (Munich: Albrecht Knaus, 1987). The account in David Hinton, *The Films of Leni Riefenstahl* (Metuchen and London: Scarecrow Press, 1978) also contains some information from earlier interviews with Riefenstahl.

16 The Reichsmark was technically a non-convertible currency at this time, so it is impossible to calculate an accurate equivalent value in either dollars or pounds. As a guide, one dollar approximated to two and a half Reichsmarks, so the budget was of the order of $600,000 – an extraordinary and probably unprecedented sum for a documentary.

17 See Cooper C. Graham, *Leni Riefenstahl and Olympia* (Metuchen and London: Scarecrow Press, 1986). Graham has written an excellent account of the production of *Olympia* based on extensive research in the German archives. Although Riefenstahl met Graham when he was researching his book, she soon fell out with him and threatened him with several law suits if he went ahead.

18 *Goebbels Tagebuch*, 1935, Bundesarchiv, quoted in Graham, p. 19.

19 The copy in the Bundesarchiv is a draft ('Entwurf') only and is not signed by Riefenstahl, but it seems to be the form of contract that Goebbels wanted.

20 Riefenstahl gives her account of the preparations for the film in her memoirs.

21 Graham provides a detailed account of the planning for the film in *Leni Riefenstahl and Olympia*.

22 From the *Film-Kurier*, quoted in Graham, pp. 31–2.

23 Graham (pp. 66–7) quotes in full the detailed ruling laid down by the IAAF on 27 July concerning where cameras could and could not be positioned. This document is of great interest in the developing relationship between sport and film because it spells out precisely what was thought to be acceptable in 1936.

24 Today a film stock would not be considered fast unless it had a speed of more than 250 ASA.

25 Before Berlin, the Olympic Games took place over a longer period, but the sixteen-day schedule has survived ever since. The major change since Berlin is that the athletics events now take place during the second week of the Games, culminating in the relay finals and the men's marathon on the last day. In Berlin, the athletics events were held in the first week and there was a strong feeling of anti-climax when the track and field events in the main stadium came to an end.

26 *Goebbels Tagebuch*, quoted in Graham, p. 145.

27 *Goebbels Tagebuch*, quoted in Graham, p. 150. It is interesting that Graham in his analysis of the claims of financial mismanagement by the Olympia Film Company comes down on the side of the Propaganda Ministry, saying that such abuses of funds supplied from the public purse should not have been tolerated.

28 The opening credits carved in stone also proclaim that the film is dedicated to the founder of the modern Olympic Games, Baron Pierre de Coubertin, and 'To the Honour and Glory of the Youth of the World'.

29 Leni Riefenstahl, *Schönheit im Olympischen Kampf* (Berlin: 1938).

30 Barnouw, *Documentary – A History of the Non-Fiction Film*, p. 109.

31 The BBC provided the first 'live' television coverage of the Olympics for the London Games in 1948 when some events were broadcast to the eighty thousand homes which then had television sets.

32 This event was replaced by the 100 metres hurdles in 1972.

33 Owens's achievement was unique in track and field until Carl Lewis repeated his record by winning four gold medals in the Los Angeles Games of 1984. This outstanding achievement was by a man who in his youth had seen Owens as a role model. The 1984 Games were marred by the Soviet-led boycott which deprived Lewis of some of his toughest competition. At Seoul in 1988, Lewis won three gold medals, taking a silver in the 200 metres and missing by a few hundredths of a second the opportunity to repeat Owens's achievement for a remarkable second time.

34 Two participants in the Games, Godfrey Brown and Godfrey Rampling, were able to describe the event to the author on film in 1984, nearly fifty years after the Games, with almost every detail exact. The interviews were used in *The Games in Question*, produced by Flashback Television for Channel Four in 1984.

35 Kitei Son was an ardent Korean nationalist who bitterly resented having to run in the vest of the nation then occupying his country. As a tribute fifty years later in 1986, the IOC officially changed the record of his victory to that of his Korean name, Sohn Kee-chung, and the gold medal was reallocated from Japan to Korea. In the Seoul Games of 1988, Sohn Kee-chung carried the Olympic flame into the stadium in the Opening Ceremony.

36 There are no women in this opening sequence, since the Olympic Village was all-male. The women competitors had separate dormitories elsewhere in Berlin.

37 The Modern Pentathlon events not included in the film were fencing and swimming. The swimming event, which was watched by Hitler, was certainly filmed but it seems that Laforgue's camera developed a fault that day and the material might have been unusable.

38 As the German swimmer Sietas is pulled out of the pool in wide shot, it is possible to see Riefenstahl arguing fiercely with Hans Ertl in the bottom left of the frame.

39 Hans Ertl's detailed accounts of how he achieved some of these effects, including underwater slow-motion shots and changes of exposure and focus below the water are quoted in Graham, pp. 115–18.

40 Riefenstahl did not receive this award from the IOC until 1948.

41 These claims have largely been accepted by Transit-Film, on the one part, who came to a secret deal with her in 1964, and by the IOC on the other, who claim that they have owned the event of the Olympic Games since 1896 but do not claim any rights on the exploitation of the film record of the 1936 Games.

42 All rights in Olympic material now revert directly to the IOC between one and four years after an Olympic Games. In the future there can be none of the confusion about rights and exploitation that has dogged *Olympia*.

43 See John Huntley, 'The XIV Olympiad', in *Film Industry*, 12 August 1948.

CREDITS

· ·

Olympia

Germany
1938
German première
20 April 1938
Part II released
3 June 1938
Producer
Leni Riefenstahl
Production manager
Walter Traut
Financial manager
Walter Groskopf
Unit managers
Arthur Kiekebusch, Rudolph
Fichtner, Konstantin
Boenisch
Director
Leni Riefenstahl
Prologue photography
Willy Zielke
**Principal photography
(black and white)**
Hans Ertl, Walter Frentz,
Gustav 'Guzzi' Lantschner,
Heinz von Jaworsky, Kurt
Neubert, Hans Scheib

Additional photography
Andor von Barsy, Wilfried
Basse, Josef Dietze, Edmund
Epkens, Fritz von Friedl,
Hans Gottschalk, Richard
Groschopp, Wilhelm
Hameister, Wolf Hart,
Hasso Hartnagel, Walter
Hege, Eberhard von der
Heyden, Albert Höcht, Paul
Holzki, Werner
Hundhausen, Hugo von
Kaweczynski, Herbert
Kebelmann, Sepp Ketterer,
Wolfgang Kiepenheuer,
Albery Kling, Ernst
Kunstmann, Leo de
Laforgue, Alexander von
Lagorio, Eduardo Lamberti,
Otto Lantschner, Waldemar
Lemke, Georg Lemki, C.A.
Linke, Erich Nitzschmann,
Albert Schattmann, Wilhelm
Schmidt, Hugo Schulze, Leo
Schwedler, Alfred Siegert,
Wilhelm Georg Siehm,
Ernst Sorge, Helmuth von
Stvolinski, Karl Vass.
Music
Herbert Windt
Music performed by
Berlin Philharmonic
Orchestra
Conducted by Herbert
Windt
Editors
Leni Riefenstahl, Max
Michel, Johannes Lüdke,
Arnfried Heyne
Assembly editor
Erna Peters
Assistant editors
Wolfgang Brüning, Otto
Lantschner
Sets
Robert Herlth

**Special photographic
effects for torchbearer's
run**
Team Svend Noldan
Newsreel material
Ufa, Tobis-Melo,
Paramount, Fox
Sound recordist
Siegfried Schulze
Dubbing mixer
Hermann Storr
Narrators
Paul Laven, Rolf Wernicke,
Henri Nannen, Johannes
Pagels
English narrator
Howard Marshall
218 minutes
19,608 feet
**Original German version
title**
Olympische Spiele

The print in the National
Film Archive derives from
material donated by the
Imperial War Museum,
London, in 1949.
Presentation of this film
has been made possible
by a grant from
Eddie Kulukundis.

BIBLIOGRAPHY

· ·

1 Books

Berg-Pan, Renata, *Leni Riefenstahl* (Boston: Twayne, 1980).

Fest, Joachim C., *Hitler* (London: Weidenfeld and Nicolson, 1974).

Graham, Cooper C., *Leni Riefenstahl and Olympia* * (Metuchen and London: Scarecrow Press, 1986).

Hart-Davis, Duff, *Hitler's Games* (London: Century, 1986).

Hinton, David, *The Films of Leni Riefenstahl* (Metuchen and London: Scarecrow Press, 1978).

Hull, David Stewart, *Film in the Third Reich* (New York: Simon and Schuster, 1973).

Furhammar, Leif and Isaksson, Folke, *Politics and Film* (London: Studio Vista, 1971).

Mandell, Richard D., *The Nazi Olympics* (New York: Ballantine, 1971).

Riefenstahl, Leni, *Schönheit im Olympischen Kampf* (Berlin: 1938). Republished with an Introduction by Monique Berlioux and Kevin Brownlow in 1983.

Riefenstahl, Leni, *Memoiren* (Munich: Albrecht Knaus, 1987), to be published in English in 1992.

Sarris, Andrew (ed.), *Interviews with Film Directors* (Indianapolis: Bobbs Merrill, 1968).

2 Articles

Downing, Taylor, 'The First Olympic Games on Film', in *Olympic Review* no. 227, September 1986.

Gardner, Robert, 'Can the Will Triumph?', in *Film Comment*, vol. 3 no. 1, Winter 1965.

Gregor, Ulrich, 'A Comeback for Leni Riefenstahl', in *Film Comment*, vol. 3 no. 1, Winter 1965.

Gunston, David, 'Leni Riefenstahl', in *Film Quarterly*, vol. 14 no. 1, Fall 1960.

Hitchens, Gordon, 'An Interview with a Legend', in *Film Comment*, vol. 3 no. 1, Winter 1965.

Loiperdinger, Martin and Culbert, David, 'Leni Riefenstahl, the SA, and the Nazi Party Rally Films, Nuremberg 1933–34: "Sieg des Glaubens" and "Triumph des Willens"', in *The Historical Journal of Film, Radio and Television*, vol. 8 no. 1, 1988.

Sontag, Susan, 'Fascinating Fascism', in *New York Review of Books*, 6 February 1975, reprinted in Sontag, *Under the Sign of Saturn* (New York: Farrar Straus Giroux, 1980).